VOTER TURNOUT IN WESTERN EUROPE

since 1945

Rafael López Pintor
Maria Gratschew

with
Tim Bittiger, Andrew Ellis, Pippa Norris,
Richard Rose, Nina Seppälä

Voter Turnout in Western Europe

© International Institute for Democracy and Electoral Assistance 2004

International IDEA publications are independent of specific national or political interests. Views expressed in this publication do not necessarily represent the views of International IDEA, its Board or its Council members. Maps created for this publication in order to add clarity to the text do not imply any judgement on the part of the Institute on the legal status of any territory or the endorsement of any boundaries, nor does the placement or size of any country or territory reflect a political view of the Institute.

Applications for permission to reproduce or translate all or any part of this publication should be made to:

Publications Office
International IDEA
SE -103 34 Stockholm
Sweden

International IDEA encourages dissemination of its work and will promptly respond to requests for permission to reproduce or translate its publications.

Graphic design by: Holmberg Design AB, Stockholm, Sweden
Printed by: Elanders Infologistics Väst AB, Mölnlycke 2004

ISBN 91-85391-00-X

Contents

Preface *Karen Fogg* 5
Acknowledgements 6
Methodology and Types of Electoral Systems 7
Acronyms 7
Introduction *Andrew Ellis* 8

Part I: Current Issues in Voter Turnout

1. Stages in the Electoral History of Western Europe *Rafael López Pintor* 13
2. Voter Turnout in the European Union Member Countries *Richard Rose* 17
3. Compulsory Voting in Western Europe *Maria Gratschew* 25
4. Women and the Vote in Western Europe *Nina Seppälä* 33
5. Innovative Technology and its Impact on Electoral Processes *Tim Bittiger* 37
6. Will New Technology Boost Turnout?
Experiments in e-Voting and All-Postal Voting in British Local Elections *Pippa Norris* 41

Figure 2.1. Average Turnout in Elections in the EU Member Countries, 1945–2002 18
Figure 2.2. Turnout in Presidential and Parliamentary Elections Compared 19
Figure 2.3. Influences on Voter Turnout in the EU Member Countries 21
Figure 2.4. Turnout in Elections to the European Parliament, by Country, 1979–99 22
Figure 2.5. Influences on Turnout in Elections to the European Parliament, 1979–99 22
Figure 3.1. Voter Turnout at National Parliamentary Elections in Western Europe, and the Practice of Compulsory Voting 27
Figure 3.2. Sanctions for Failure to Vote 30
Figure 4.1. When Women Gained the Suffrage 34
Figure 4.2. The Gender Gap in Voter Turnout 35
Figure 6.1. Social Profile of the Online Community, European Union Member Countries, 1996–2000 43
Figure 6.2. Percentage Change in Turnout in the May 2003 British Local Election Pilot Schemes 46
Figure 6.3. Reported Voting Participation by Age Group in the May 2003 British Local Election Pilot Schemes 47

Part II: Voter Turnout Country by Country

Electoral System, Voter Turnout by Type of Election and Basic Election Data, *Maria Gratschew*

Austria 56
Belgium 57
Denmark 58
Finland 59
France 60
Germany 61
Greece 62
Iceland 63
Ireland 64

Italy	65
Luxembourg	66
Malta	67
Netherlands	68
Norway	69
Portugal	70
Spain	71
Sweden	72
Switzerland	73
United Kingdom	74

Part III: The International IDEA Database: Voter Turnout from 1945 to 2003

Definitions	78
Parliamentary Elections, 1945–2003	79
Presidential Elections, 1945–2003	85
European Parliament Elections, 1979–99	87
Ranking Table of Average Voter Turnout by Country, Western Europe: National Parliamentary Elections, 1945–2003	90
Ranking Table of Average Voter Turnout by Country, Western Europe: Presidential Elections, 1945–2003	90
Ranking Table of Average Voter Turnout by Country, Western Europe: Elections to the European Parliament, 1979–99	90
Sources	91
The Contributors	92

Preface

Electoral participation is in general falling, at least as measured by voter turnout. Rising levels of public apathy or cynicism are of growing concern in both newer and older democracies, and are a particular focus of concern in Western Europe. At the same time, there are continuing obstacles and disincentives to participation that could be diminished by adapting electoral systems or encouraging easier electoral access for all. Not enough is yet known about which practical measures are effective in encouraging turnout, and which are not. Nor are the factors which breed apathy and discontent with democratic institutions themselves sufficiently understood.

There are currently very few tools available to assist the informed consideration of turnout questions. To follow the worldwide Voter Turnout Database, IDEA is pleased to present this Regional Report on Turnout in Western Europe, which is timed to coincide with the 2004 elections to the European Parliament. The Report brings together an unrivalled set of data on parliamentary, presidential and European elections in the region. It amasses the information necessary to analyse the gap between turnout in national elections and European elections, on which further work is planned by IDEA. It analyses the impact of factors affecting voter turnout trends in the region generally, ranging from choice of polling day through electoral system choice to longevity of democracy. It considers the effects of compulsory voting and of the successes and limitations of the use of new technology in encouraging turnout.

This Report is designed to provide all those engaged in the turnout debate with the basis for the development of new insights and policy recommendations. It is a step within IDEA's programme of work to develop practical knowledge on voter turnout. It puts forward ideas, poses questions, and tests some answers against the hard data which it provides. I hope that it will make a contribution to the continuing debate on participation and democracy.

Karen Fogg
Secretary-General

Acknowledgements

A great number of organizations and individuals have made this unprecedented collection of voter turnout data possible–first and foremost the electoral management bodies that responded to our requests so quickly and willingly. Professor Rafael López Pintor of the Universidad Autónoma de Madrid and Maria Gratschew of International IDEA, who are the joint lead authors for this regional report, worked together previously on Voter Turnout since 1945: A Global Report. Their ambition to develop the Voter Turnout Project into a systematic methodology and a fundamental part of the programme work has resulted in this regional report as well as the two earlier global reports on electoral participation.

This regional report is based on work done on voter turnout over several years. Many colleagues and external writers have contributed with substantive comments and expertise. Under the supervision of my predecessors, Professor Reg Austin and Vijay Patidar, International IDEA's Elections Team developed into a highly valued programme with products and methodologies of a high standard. Kate Sullivan, Therese Laanela and Nina Seppälä all helped to lay the groundwork for this and the global reports on electoral participation. Nadia Handal Zander and Eve Johansson have also helped in the production of this report, and Richard Desjardins from Stockholm University is responsible for the statistical work presented here. In addition, International IDEA wishes to thank the following individuals and organizations for their help in providing data and information:

Austrian Ministry of Interior, Election Office
Belgian Ministry of Interior
Cyprus Central Election Service
Danish Ministry of Interior and Health
Finnish Ministry of Justice
French Constitutional Council and Ministry of Interior
German Federal Returning Officer
Greek Ministry of Interior and Embassy of the Hellenic Republic in Sweden
Icelandic Ministry of Justice and Ecclesiastical Affairs
Irish Ministry of Environment and Local Governance
Italian Ministry of Interior
Luxembourg Chamber of Deputies
Maltese Electoral Office
Netherlands Ministry of Interior and Kingdom Relations, National Election Board
Norwegian Ministry of Local Government and Regional Development
Portuguese Ministry of Internal Administration (STAPE, Secretariado Tecnico para Assuntos para Processo Eleitoral)

Spanish Ministry of Interior
Swedish Election Authority
Swiss Federal Chancery, Section of Political Rights
UK Electoral Commission
University of Florence, Department for Political Science and Sociology (on Italy)

Herman Beun
Sarah Birch
André Blais
Susanne Caarls
Maria del Carmen Alanis
Konrad Ginther
Gunnar Helgi Kristinsson
Anna Katz
Wilfried Kindli
Lotta Lann
Stina Larserud
Lawrence LeDuc
Frances Lesser
Tom Lodge
Rafael López Pintor
Pippa Norris
Jon Pammett
Andrew Reynolds
Richard Rose
Antonio Spinelli
Sara Staino
Ólafur Stefansson
Markku Suksi
Hans-Urs Wili

We also take the opportunity to acknowledge gratefully all those who have been involved in the work on previous Voter Turnout reports.

Andrew Ellis
Head of Electoral Processes
International IDEA

Methodology and Types of Electoral System

The aim of International IDEA's Voter Turnout Project is to provide up-to-date and reliable information about voter turnout around the world. Some trends are highlighted and conclusions are drawn in this report, but International IDEA does not aim to explain or to prove definitively why turnout differs between countries and across regions. The data should be seen as a basis for further research; additional correlations and comparisons can be drawn on the basis of the individual user's particular needs and interests.

This particular report has a regional focus. Western Europe has been chosen on the basis of the many debates going on in the region about a possible decline in voter turnout. Among the regions of the world it has traditionally had some of the highest average levels of turnout, and a discussion of a declining turnout in Western Europe is therefore very interesting and highly relevant.

Choosing the Elections
The Voter Turnout database includes elections held since 1945. The criteria for including elections in this report are:
- the elections were held after 1945 but before 30 June 2003;
- the elections were for national political office in independent nation states;
- there was a degree of competitiveness, that is, more than one party contested the election, or one party and independent candidates contested the election, or the election was only contested by independent candidates. Within this 'grey area' we have erred on the side of inclusion (for instance, in Iceland there has on occasion been only one candidate for a presidential election) and, at least where data is available, we have included the turnout figures and explanatory variables in the tables; and
- the franchise was universal. However, for purposes of comparison we have included in this regional report the following elections when women were excluded from voting: Liechtenstein before 1986, Switzerland before 1971, Greece before 1956 and Belgium in 1948. In these cases, the voting age population figure only includes men.

This particular report covers the following 19 West European countries: Austria, Belgium, Denmark, Finland, France, Germany, Greece, Iceland, Ireland, Italy, Luxembourg, Malta, the Netherlands, Norway, Portugal, Spain, Sweden, Switzerland and the United Kingdom. Liechtenstein is also discussed in the relevant chapters but is not included in the statistical summaries.

Sources
Many researchers have difficulty obtaining information about registration figures and voter turnout rates. International IDEA's extensive network of electoral management bodies (EMBs) around the world has made it possible for us, in most cases, to use the official data compiled in different countries as our main source of information. When this source has not been available we have used information from government departments, universities or research institutes to find the necessary data on elections.

Types of Electoral System
First past the post (FPTP) The simplest form of plurality majority electoral system, using single-member districts. The winning candidate is the one who gains more votes than any other candidate, but not necessarily a majority of votes.
List proportional representation (List PR) involves each party presenting a list of candidates to the electorate. In its simplest form, closed list PR, voters vote for a party, and parties receive seats in proportion to their overall share of the national vote. Winning candidates are taken from the lists. Open list PR systems give voters the opportunity to vote for individual candidates as well as for a party. Parties receive seats in proportion to the overall share of the vote. The individual candidates that receive the most support are elected to those seats.
Mixed member proportional (MMP) Systems in which a proportion of the parliament (usually half) is elected from plurality majority districts, while the remaining members are chosen from PR lists. Under MMP the PR seats compensate for any disproportion produced by the district seat result.
Single transferable vote (STV) A preferential PR system used in multi-member districts. To gain election, candidates must exceed a specified quota of first-preference votes. Voters' preferences are reallocated to other continuing candidates if a candidate is excluded or if an elected candidate has a surplus.
Two-round system (TRS) A plurality majority system in which a second election is held if no candidate achieves an absolute majority of votes in the first election.

Acronyms
EU   European Union
EVM   Electronic voting machine
GDP   Gross domestic product
MP   Member of Parliament
NGO   Non-governmental organization
PR   Proportional representation

Introduction

Andrew Ellis

This report on voter turnout in Western Europe is designed to bring together and make widely available the data collected by International IDEA and to promote discussion on issues relating to voter turnout and participation. The report covers the 15 member states of the European Union before 2004, plus Iceland, Malta, Norway and Switzerland. Since 1945, more than 300 elections have been held in these countries. This report includes statistics up to and including most of the elections held in 2003—a total of 299 general elections, 43 presidential elections and five European Parliament elections (in addition to those held on the occasion of successive enlargement of the EU). The statistics cover the period up to 2003, including most of the elections held during 2003.

Voter turnout is not a new issue, as Rafael López Pintor demonstrates in his chapter surveying the development of the franchise. However, it has come to be much more extensively debated in Western Europe during the 1990s. Examples of declining turnout are brought up at one national election after another, with particular concern being expressed after spectacular drops such as the 12 per cent drop in the UK between the general elections of 1997 and 2001. But, as Richard Rose asks in his chapter, do these elections provide evidence to support a general theory that turnout in Western Europe is falling? If so, is it then valid to infer that public interest in democratic participation has declined, or even that the general public's commitment to democracy is waning?

The report demonstrates that average turnout for elections to national parliaments in Western Europe has indeed declined since the early to mid-1990s. When looking at individual countries, only six of those included in this report experienced an increase in turnout at the most recent national parliamentary election compared with the previous one, while 13 countries showed a fall. There is still debate as to whether this fall reflects a significant long-term shift in the willingness of Western European electors to participate in democracy through the act of voting. There are, however, consistent findings that turnout is related to political systems, frameworks and institutions: for example, proportional representation systems tend to be associated with higher turnout, while the call for citizens to visit the polling station 'too frequently' to participate in elections and/or referenda may depress turnout.

This report is published to coincide with the 2004 elections to the European Parliament. Turnout is an issue at every European Parliament election, and 2004 is no exception. There was a decline in turnout in 11 of the 15 member states between the 1994 and 1999 European elections, and many countries are now worried that turnout will fall further in 2004. If this fear is realized, it will have political implications, impacting perhaps on the perceived legitimacy of the European Parliament. Are lack of interest and the perception that its role is limited a cause of low turnout? Or will a low turnout lead in turn to declining interest in and a limited role for the European Parliament?

The accession of 10 new member states to the EU in May 2004 will demonstrate how willing the citizens of 25 countries are to vote simultaneously for members of one parliamentary body. Will this in itself affect turnout? It has been suggested, for example, that commitment to the institutions of democracy may be reflected in high turnout reflecting initial excitement when a transition from authoritarianism takes place, but fall after the euphoria has worn off and only increase again as the time over which democracy has been in place increases. Are harmonization issues important? For example, some of the new member states have included turnout thresholds in their electoral systems: if turnout does not pass a specified level, the election is invalid and has to be held again. Will these thresholds cause political problems if turnout does not reach the required level—perhaps not just once but several times in succession? Is there a case for a pan-European election law for European Parliamentary elections, and would this be a practical political suggestion?

Of the 19 countries covered in this report, six EU member states (Austria, France, Finland, Portugal and Ireland) plus Iceland (where presidential elections are often uncontested) have presidential elections as well as national and European parliamentary elections. In these six countries, presidential elections show a 5 per cent lower average turnout than parliamentary elections. However, this is not a global pattern. One explanation for this may be that many of Europe's presidents only have the role of head of state in a parliamentary system, and that the incentive to vote in a presidential election is very different in a presidential system where the elected president is also the head of executive government.

The perception that turnout is declining has led to a flurry of debate as politicians, election administrators and commentators express concern. One response that has been proposed to the 'turnout question' is a reversal of the slow decline both in the number of countries which practise compulsory voting and in the level of enforcement in those countries where voting remains compulsory. As Maria Gratschew indicates in her chapter, the political acceptability of this as an answer to the problem may be questionable, especially in contexts where previous non-democratic regimes made voting compulsory.

Introduction

The decision to participate or not is, of course, ultimately a personal one; different people, and different groups in society, may take this decision in different ways. The differences in turnout between men and women are explored by Nina Seppälä in her chapter, tracking the history of the women's franchise and looking at some gender differences in voting patterns. This debate may encourage more electoral authorities to collect electoral data which disaggregates the turnout of men and of women.

Remote voting and electronic voting have become prominent on the agenda in Europe as politicians and electoral authorities attempt to attract young voters and busy voters by enabling them to vote at the supermarket, over the Internet or by using their mobile phone. The Council of Europe is in the final stage of drafting recommendations on e-voting. There have been several tests of wider facilities for remote voting, while the UK and some Swiss cantons have taken e-voting one step further and actually tried it. Pippa Norris writes in her chapter about the experience of the UK pilots, and Tim Bittiger about this kind of technology in general.

The assessment of remote voting and e-voting initiatives will address the security and cost implications of their introduction. They will also address their effectiveness. This is not just a question of plain numbers: is it necessarily positive if an increase in overall turnout is achieved because the turnout of some groups in the society increased disproportionately? In addition, as Richard Rose has pointed out, measures to encourage turnout may produce other effects which may not be considered so desirable. There seems little doubt, for example, that elections conducted entirely by post can increase turnout substantially, but do they also have a negative effect on electoral integrity, for instance, through the opportunities they may present for the 'head of the family' to vote for the whole family, or even for outright fraud? And, if there is a problem of trust in institutions, will innovations that demand the confidence of citizens in the integrity and accurate functioning of a 'black box' mechanism necessarily help?

Is there a connection between the role of the media and electoral turnout? There is debate as to whether the existence of more and more television channels, newspapers and radio stations gives people access to more in-depth coverage of elections and politics. Can the vast increase in the choice of media be leading instead to ignorance of politics, lack of interest and apathy as people 'choose other channels'?

Turnout may also be affected as societies become more mobile. Electoral registration may be a much easier exercise when most citizens live at the same address year after year. Election administrators are facing challenges to devise effective ways of enabling both long-term migrants and short-term travellers to participate in elections. The effect of administrative changes may be important. Making polling day a public holiday may increase turnout; holding elections during periods when many electors take a major holiday may have the reverse effect. Efforts to ensure ease of voting for the disabled, pregnant women and the elderly may increase turnout in addition to promoting equality of electoral access.

There is of course a difference between low and declining turnout. A low turnout means a constant low turnout. Turnout in Switzerland is among the lowest in Western Europe: does this mean that the Swiss are dissatisfied with their model of citizens' democracy? Or does the low turnout in Swiss general elections reflect the limited governmental change that has usually resulted from these elections, while most citizens also participate in votes on those referenda and initiatives which they individually find of personal interest and importance?

On the other hand, a decline in turnout indicates change, and could indicate dissatisfaction or a change of perception of the impact of the political system—although this link cannot be assumed.

When any subject is fiercely debated, there is a particular need for reliable data and analysis. International IDEA has already published and maintains a worldwide database of voter turnout, available electronically at <http://www.idea.int> and in handbook form. This report follows on from the database to provide an easily accessible source of data for election administrators and designers as well as for the community of political analysts, and to promote analysis and the exchange of ideas in the field. IDEA has also established an Expert Group on Voter Turnout to encourage further identification of those factors which have a real effect on turnout, positive or negative, and those which do not. Pippa Norris has written that political institutions and legal rules are strongly and significantly associated with voter participation: some of the factors affecting turnout will thus be within the control of legislators, electoral system designers or election administrators. Others, such as social or cultural factors, will not. Analyses of these may better be used to inform the expectations of electoral administrators, participants and commentators in advance of elections.

IDEA is seeking to develop tools which can provide those participating in debate about change and improvement in democracy and electoral arrangements with solid information and knowledge on turnout issues. This report will serve its purpose if it helps to stimulate both work towards such tools and wider debate on participation and democracy itself.

Part I:
Current Issues in Voter Turnout

1. Stages in the Electoral History of Western Europe

Rafael López Pintor

The history of voter enfranchisement and universal suffrage is part of the history of the quest for and achievement of civil rights and political freedoms. The demand for voter enfranchisement cannot generally be separated from a broader demand for social equality and the general struggle for rights and freedoms.

It is a story of social conflict. The quest for universal suffrage in Europe was an important aspect of the social and political emancipation of newly emerging social classes during the 19th century—first an urban middle class, then the industrial proletariat—and then, by extension, the transformation of the peasantry. The banner of universal suffrage was first raised by the liberal movement of the 19th century, and later in the same century by the socialist parties. The development of trade unions and political parties implied a move away from absolute political control by crowned rulers and landowning aristocracies: trade unions and political parties were crucially important in the realization of the demand for universal suffrage. Later, from the last quarter of the 19th century onwards, came the struggle against the industrial bourgeoisie and governmental bureaucratic elites towards increased general social and political autonomy.

Landmarks for Freedom
In the West European region as a whole, several landmarks can be identified on the road to full or universal voter enfranchisement. The first seeds were sown by the

Part I: Current Issues in Voter Turnout

English Bill of Rights of 1689 and the French Revolution, especially the latter, which had an impact on many other countries both in and outside Europe. Second, although the liberal revolutions which took place across Europe in 1848 were unsuccessful, the ideas which inspired them gained ground during the nineteenth century. Third, there was the period between the First and Second World Wars when voting rights were legally recognized for large sectors of the population, especially women. Finally, there was the period after the Second World War when the right to vote was made truly universal—in practice if not by law-thanks to the democratic commitment of the victorious Allies and the unprecedented socio-economic prosperity which was built in the post-war period.

The fight for rights and freedoms throughout the 19th and 20th centuries in Western Europe had a historical antecedent in the signing of the Bill of Rights in England in 1689, which the English elite imposed on the new King and Queen of England, William III of Orange and his wife Mary, after the ousting of King James II, a Catholic. The Bill declared the rights and liberties of the subjects, and settled the succession of the crown. It was followed by the Act of Toleration of 1690 on religious practices and the revival of the earlier Triennial Act preventing the King from dissolving Parliament at will and establishing that general elections should be held every three years. The franchise at the time was however limited to the landowning aristocracy and the upper levels of an urban bourgeoisie, and included only males in their mid-20s and over. This predated by almost 100 years the revolution fought by the European émigrés in North America which led to independence in 1776 and laid the foundation of an electoral democracy in the United States of America with the constitution of 1787, just two years before the French Revolution of 1789. In France, universal suffrage was granted to adult French men in 1848 by the February revolution which toppled Louis Philippe. As a consequence, Louis Napoleon Bonaparte was elected president on the basis of his name alone. The Paris Commune of 1871—an attempted proletarian revolution—ruled that municipal councillors could be elected by universal suffrage. However, regime changes in different countries brought reversals from time to time of some of the advances achieved, for example in France.

Gender, Property, Age, and Education as Barriers to Voter Enfranchisement

Between 1870 and the 1940s, universal suffrage was established for males in Austria, Denmark, Italy, France, Germany, Spain and Switzerland. During the same time period, in other countries the male suffrage already established was further extended to practically the entire male adult population—Belgium, Finland, Norway, the United Kingdom and Sweden. While in many of these countries women's right to vote was legally established after the First World War in recognition of the supportive role played by women during the conflict, in some countries the gender barrier was the last to fall after a century of struggle for the female franchise. There are states in Europe where women were only enfranchised a few decades ago, most notably Switzerland in 1971 and the micro-state of Liechtenstein in 1984.

The earliest countries in Europe to give legal recognition to women's right to vote were Finland in 1906 and Norway in 1913. The struggle for women's suffrage was particularly intense in the UK, with the Chartist movement demanding the suffrage for women from the 1840s, followed by the Labour Party after it was founded in 1900. Socialist parties in many other European countries also incorporated the right to vote for men and women alike into their programmes. The inter-war period and the aftermath of the Second World War saw women being given the right to vote in many European countries—Austria, Czechoslovakia, Germany, Poland, Sweden and the UK in 1918-1919; Hungary in 1920; Spain in 1931; France in 1944; Italy in 1945; and Greece in 1952 (see chapter 4). In general, it can be said that barriers to enfranchisement based on property were lowered in the countries of Europe during the late 19th century, age barriers had came down by the early 20th century, and education and gender barriers only finally disappeared by the middle of the 20th century or even later. Needless to say, these are general trends within which each country has taken its own road towards universal suffrage, setting its own landmarks.

Once male suffrage was granted, the first barrier to the exercise of the new right was a property barrier. Although male suffrage was granted throughout Europe in the revolutionary years after 1848, voter eligibility was mostly limited by property or tax qualifications until much later in the century, and in some cases well into the 20th century, when voting rights were extended beyond the boundaries of the propertied classes. 'Universal' male suffrage actually fell well short of being universal. In Great Britain, for example, the property qualification was called the 'lodger' vote as it implied the ownership of a freehold or the occupation of premises of a certain value. In Spain, where 'universal male suffrage' was first established by the Cadiz Constitution of 1812, this was in actuality a right for the bourgeoisie and was only extended to the wider propertied classes in 1837. The wider suffrage after 1837 was called the censitary vote, which could only be exercised by citizens who paid taxes above a certain amount (censo). Only 3.5 per cent of the population could vote under this system, which was a relatively high proportion within the European context of the time: it was similar to the percentage in Great Britain and the Netherlands, and much higher than that of Belgium, where 1 per cent of the population were actually able to vote, or France under Louis Philippe, where the figure was 0.67 per cent. The 1844 coup d'état in Spain reversed the situation by once again limiting the exercise of universal suffrage to the upper bourgeoisie. With the restoration of democracy during the last quarter of the 19th century there was a progressive reduction of the tax threshold above which the right to vote applied. Property limitations were less severe in countries like Greece, where the 1844 constitution established universal suffrage for those holding land property. Due to the predominance of small peasant ownership, the suffrage in Greece now became almost universal.

A second barrier to the right to vote was age. In general, a minimum voting age between 23 and 30 was the rule until later in the 20th century, when it was set at 18. At the beginning of the 20th century, it was 24 in Austria, 25 in Belgium, Prussia, the Netherlands and Norway, and 30 in Denmark. In Sweden the voting age for general elections was lowered to 21 from 23 only in 1945. In the UK, where women had been granted the right to vote in 1918, the voting age for women then was 30; it was reduced to 21 in 1928, and the voting age for both men and women was further lowered to 18 in 1969. In France, the right to vote at age 18 was also established in 1969. Most recently, the German state *(Land)* of Lower Saxony *(Niedersachsen)* lowered the voting age in local elections to 16 in 1995. Other German states have since followed, and three Austrian states *(Länder)* have also introduced a voting age of 16 in local elections. In contrast, the voting age for elections to the Italian Senate remains at 25. Also until late in the 20th century, a common qualification for the exercise of the right to vote was literacy: voters should know how to read and write.

Following these reflections on the history of voting rights in Western Europe, some brief comments on the present-day frontiers in the advance of the actual practice of universal suffrage are appropriate.

Among the major challenges are the following:

- *making voting easier* for the elderly and the disabled. Postal voting and easier access to polling stations are making voting easier for the disabled, and an international association has been set up to promote this cause;
- *improving the efficiency* of voting from abroad. A cross-national study of nationals voting from abroad has recently been carried out under the auspices of the national electoral authority of Mexico, the Instituto Federal Electoral (IFE). An assessment of the experiences of postal voting in Spain, Portugal and Austria, and of a mixed system in Sweden, has also been conducted (<http://www.universidadabierta.edu.mx>);
- *allowing non-nationals who are resident* to vote in local elections in European Union countries (European Commission 2002); and
- *the assessment of the impact of electronic voting on participation,* considering questions of efficiency and the quality of the vote, and possible drawbacks for example in the area of electoral integrity (see chapter 5).

References and Further Reading

European Commission, *Report from the Commission to the European Parliament and the Council on the Application of Directive 94/80EC on the Right to Vote and to stand as a Candidate in Municipal Elections* (Brussels, May 2002)

Universidad Abierta, <http://www.universidadabierta.edu.mx>

Inter-Parliamentary Union, <http://www.ipu.org>

2. Voter Turnout in the European Union Member Countries[1]

Richard Rose

Western Europe has more long-established democracies than any other region of the world. Free elections have been held without interruption for more than a century in countries such as Belgium, Denmark, France, Ireland, Luxembourg, the Netherlands, Sweden and the United Kingdom. Free elections were introduced by the end of the First World War in Austria, Germany, Finland and Italy, but interrupted by periods of undemocratic rule. Even the relative latecomers—Greece, Portugal and Spain—have had free elections for more than a quarter of a century, long enough for most adults to have enjoyed the right to vote throughout their adult lives.

Yet turnout in West European countries is not as high as democratic activists would like, and there are some signs that electors are less likely to vote today than they were a generation ago. Among the 233 national *parliamentary elections* that took place in 15 different European Union (EU) member countries up to the end of 2002 and an additional 64 national elections for the European Parliament since the Second World War, it is always possible to find examples of turnout going down or going up, and generalizations based on one country can be contradicted by generalizations drawn from another.

---

[1] This chapter analyses turnout in elections up to April 2002. It therefore excludes nine elections held subsequently, which are included in the statistical tables at the end of the book.

Part I: Current Issues in Voter Turnout

Moreover, in half a century turnout can fluctuate up as well as down. Hence, the purpose of this chapter is to review trends in turnout systematically in order to determine whether or not the electorates of many of the world's oldest democracies are losing interest in exercising their right to vote and, if so, why.

Differences Between Countries and Across Time

When the latest election results are compared across national boundaries, differences in turnout are immediately apparent. Even though a majority of electors invariably participate in their national elections, there is a big gap between the highest and lowest turnouts. The Belgian turnout of 90.6 per cent in 1999 was more than half as great again as the record low turnout of 59.4 per cent in the UK in 2001.

In parliamentary *elections* from 1945 to 2002, the average turnout in the EU member countries has been 83.0 per cent of the registered electorate. This average in fact underrepresents the proportion of the electorate who usually vote, for it is consistent with every elector voting in five out of six national elections. When a citizen is occasionally absent from the polls this is a sign not of political disaffection but of an unexpected or unwanted change in personal circumstances, such as being unexpectedly sick or on holiday on election day. Voting turnout may also be depressed by inaccuracies in the electoral register, such as the inclusion of deceased persons or those who have emigrated as still eligible to vote. In short, an overwhelming majority of citizens have voted in a majority of the elections in which they are eligible to vote.

A multi-national average conceals substantial differences between countries in the average level of turnout in each (figure 2.1). Belgium has consistently had a high turnout: in the 18 elections to the national Parliament from 1945 to 1999 an average of 92.5 per cent of the electorate participated, and turnout has never dropped below 90 per cent. In Luxembourg and Italy, almost nine-tenths of electors have usually voted. At the other end of the continuum, turnout averages 73.2 per cent in Ireland, and below 75 per cent in Portugal and France. Even here, however, to describe turnout as 'low' in a country in which three out of four voters participate in elections is misleading; it would be more accurate to describe turnout as 'less high' or simply as below the EU average.

In the past half-century turnout has varied relatively little: the standard deviation is only 8.3 per cent. In more than two-thirds of national elections, 75 per cent of the electorate votes and there is a turnout of more than 90 per cent in almost one-third of all elections. In ten of the 15 EU countries, turnout at every election in more than half a century has always been 75 per cent or higher. Only

Figure 2.1: Turnout in Elections in the EU Member Countries, 1945–2002
Figures are percentages of the registered electorate.

	Minimum	Maximum	Mean
Belgium	90.0	95.1	92.5
Austria	80.4	96.8	91.3
Compulsory, 1945–79	91.8	96.8	94.0
Semi-compulsory 1983–	80.4	92.6	86.3
Italy	81.4	93.9	89.8
1946–87	88.9	93.9	91.8
1992– (new system)	81.4	87.4	84.5
Luxembourg	86.5	91.6	89.7
Netherlands	73.2	95.6	87.2
Compulsory 1945–67	93.1	95.6	94.7
Non-compulsory 1971–	73.2	88.0	81.9
Denmark	80.6	89.9	86.0
Sweden	77.4	91.4	85.7
Germany	77.8	91.1	85.0
1949–87	78.5	91.1	87.0
1990 (reunification)	77.8	82.2	79.5
Greece	75.0	84.5	79.9
1951–64 (pre-coup)	75.0	83.0	78.5
1974–	75.0	84.5	81.0
Finland	65.3	85.1	76.0
Portugal	61.0	91.7	75.7
United Kingdom	59.4	83.6	75.2
France	60.3	82.7	74.8
4th Republic	78.8	82.7	81.1
5th Republic	60.3	81.3	72.7
Spain	68.1	79.8	73.6
Ireland	66.1	76.9	73.2
EU countries	59.4	96.8	83.0

Source: Figures supplied from the International IDEA Voter Turnout database for elections in all EU member countries from 1945 to April 2002.

once in 233 national parliamentary elections has turnout dropped below 60 per cent of the registered electorate; this happened in the UK in 2001.

Differences in turnout within countries are greater than the difference between countries. In Portugal there is a difference of 30.7 percentage points between the 1975 high, in the country's first free election, and the 1999 parliamentary election. Turnout has also varied more within the Netherlands, France and the UK than it has between the two countries with the highest and lowest turnouts over the period, Belgium and Ireland.

Changes in the rules for conducting elections or governing can affect average turnout. Since the Netherlands in 1967 repealed a law making it compulsory for registered electors to vote, turnout has fallen by an average of 12.8 percentage points. Since Austria stopped imposing a

Voter Turnout in Western Europe

federal requirement to vote (see also chapter 3), average turnout has fallen by 7.7 percentage points. The Greek regime that replaced military rule has achieved a higher average turnout than the regime that governed before the 1967 military coup. However, in France the change from the Fourth to the Fifth Republic in 1958 was accompanied by a fall in turnout. In Italy, the introduction of a new electoral system as part of a campaign against corruption was accompanied by a fall in average turnout.

In the past half-century, great changes have affected the electorates in every West European country. There has been a rise in the level of education and average income, which is associated with increased electoral participation. Concurrently, there has been a 'de-ideologization' of politics, as parties of the left and the right have tended to move towards the centre. Insofar as the clash of ideologies reflected an electorate so strongly committed to their different parties that they would be certain to turn out at every election, then a decline in ideological commitment would lead to a fall in turnout. Furthermore, some commentators have argued that declining turnout reflects a healthy apathy, as voters no longer see elections as a clash between rival camps but as a means of influencing all parties to adopt similar, moderate policies offering what most electors want.

From the end of the Second World War until 1959, turnout in the states that were EU members before 2004 averaged 84.7 per cent. In the period of economic boom between 1960 and 1973, turnout was virtually the same, 85.6 per cent. When economic conditions soured due to oil price rises, world recession and inflation, turnout was hardly affected; it averaged 83.9 per cent between 1974 and 1987. Turnout has only shown signs of falling since 1988, averaging 78.0 per cent since then.

It is a half-truth to say that turnout is falling. In eight countries—Portugal, the Netherlands, France, Austria, Finland, Italy, the United Kingdom and Luxembourg—there has been a clear downward trend in turnout, as measured by a least squares regression line.[1] However, in seven countries—Greece, Denmark, Belgium, Spain, Sweden, Germany and Ireland—fluctuations both up and down are so numerous that there is no clear trend in either direction.

The biggest and steadiest downward trend is in Portugal. Even though Portugal has a competitive party system and government often changes hands as a result of an election, there has been a trend fall in turnout of more than 3 per cent between one election and the next since free elections were introduced in 1975. In the Netherlands, a large downward trend in turnout took place following the abolition of compulsory voting in 1967. In France, the Fifth Republic has experienced a continuing fall in turnout from 77 per cent in the 1958 election to 60 per cent in the parliamentary election of 2002.

In a television age in which personalities are considered at least as important as political parties, a *presidential election* may be expected to produce a high turnout, because it is palpably a contest between individuals. However, while every pre-2004 EU member state elects a parliament, popular election of the president occurs in only five countries. Where the head of state is a monarch, no election is necessary and in Italy, Germany and Greece the head of state is chosen by the national assembly rather than by direct election. Where there is a popularly elected president, the powers of the office vary greatly. They are greatest in France, where the president is superior to the prime minister, and substantial in Portugal and Finland, but in Austria and Ireland the president's political role is slight.

In France, turnout in presidential elections averages nine percentage points higher than in the first-round bal-

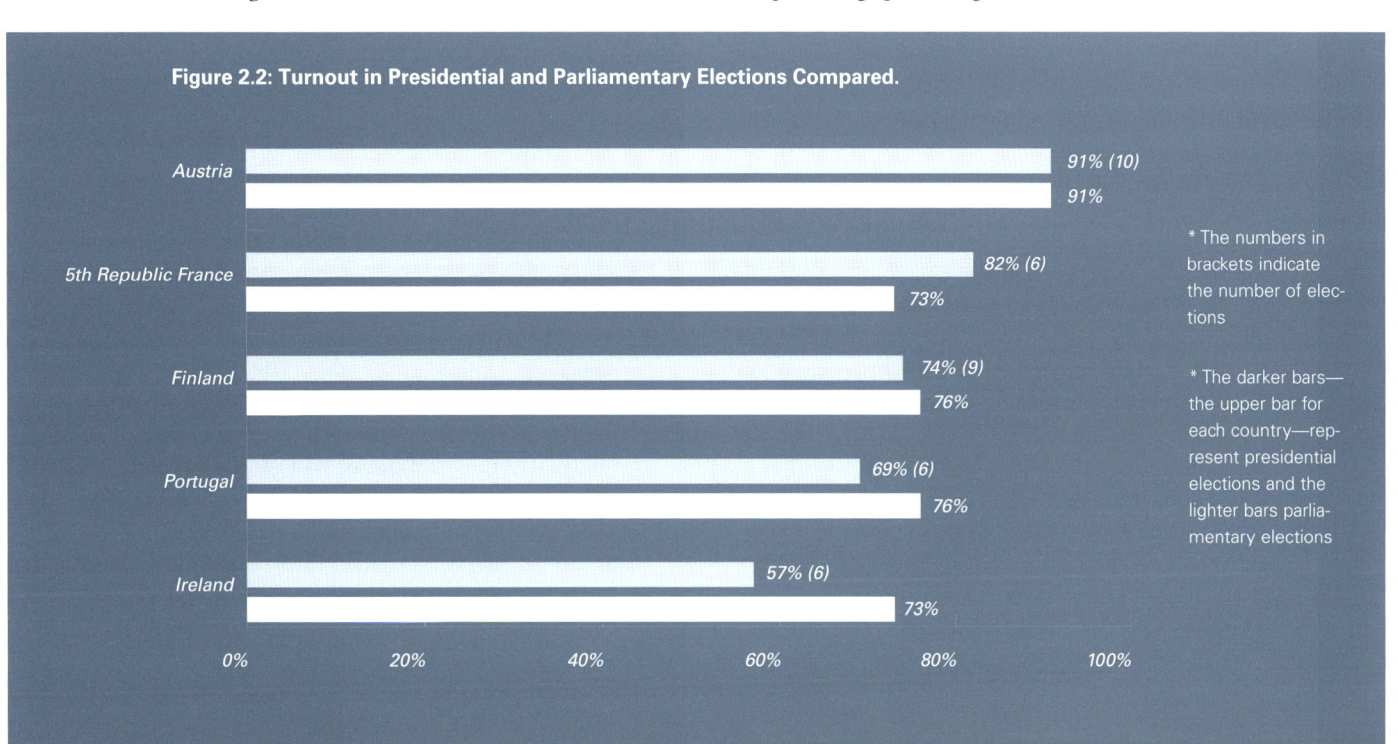

Figure 2.2: Turnout in Presidential and Parliamentary Elections Compared.

Country	Presidential	Parliamentary
Austria	91% (10)	91%
5th Republic France	82% (6)	73%
Finland	74% (9)	76%
Portugal	69% (6)	76%
Ireland	57% (6)	73%

* The numbers in brackets indicate the number of elections

* The darker bars—the upper bar for each country—represent presidential elections and the lighter bars parliamentary elections

Part I: Current Issues in Voter Turnout

lot for the National Assembly (see figure 2.2). However, the French pattern is atypical. In Ireland, where the office is sometimes filled without a contest because there is inter-party agreement about who should hold the ceremonial post, turnout for presidential elections averages 16 percentage points less than the average for elections to the Dail (Parliament). In Portugal, presidential elections produce a turnout 7 percentage points lower than elections to the National Assembly, and there is a significant downward trend. In the first Portuguese presidential election in 1976 three-quarters of the electorate voted, while in 2001 the turnout was even lower than that for the US presidential elections, at 50.0 per cent.

Explanations of Turnout

In Western Europe, the *electoral system* usually reflects laws enacted by a coalition government that depends on two, three or even four parties for support and, as coalitions vary between countries, so too do electoral arrangements. Political scientists have taken advantage of this fact to formulate the following hypotheses. Election turnout will be higher if:

- *Members of parliament* (MPs) *are elected by proportional representation* (PR). In PR elections, once support for a party exceeds a real or implicit threshold of five per cent or less, every vote cast for it helps the voters' choice get into the parliament. By contrast, in first-past-the-post elections, the winner needs just a plurality of the vote, thus causing many votes to be 'wasted'. Advocates of PR claim that it raises turnout by reducing the percentage of wasted votes. Of the 15 EU member countries before 2004, 11 have a PR electoral system and two (the UK and France) do not. Germany and Italy have mixed member proportional (MMP) systems.
- *Voting is compulsory.* Making voting compulsory ought to make turnout higher than it is in countries where it is voluntary. However, the obligation to vote usually involves 'soft compulsion', for penalties can be light or not enforced. Moreover, even if voting is voluntary, many electors may have internalized cultural norms of civic participation, thus reducing the impact of compulsion. Belgium, Luxembourg and Greece have consistently sought to make voting compulsory; the Netherlands had compulsory voting up to and including the 1967 election; and Austria had compulsory voting at the national level up to and including the 1979 election. Italy states that it is a duty of the citizen to vote but sanctions are not effective.
- *Elections are held on a rest day, not a workday.* If an election is held on a Saturday or Sunday, or election day is a public holiday, the free time in which employed electors can vote is greatly increased. At least one day of voting is a rest day in nine pre-2004 EU countries—Austria,

Belgium, France, Germany, Greece, Italy, Luxembourg, Portugal and Sweden. In the other six, employed electors are expected to make time to vote in addition to meeting their workday obligations.
- *Voters are closer to their representatives.* British politicians often argue that electors are closer to their representatives when votes are cast for an individual candidate in a single-member electoral district under the first-past-the-post system. However, such districts can have up to 100,000 electors, thus making personal contact 'virtual' at best, and the majority of electors often do not know the name of their MP. A measure that can be used for 'closeness' is the ratio of number of electors to number of MPs.
- *Free elections are long established.* Insofar as socialization into a democratic political system when young encourages citizens to vote, the longer a country has held free elections the more likely citizens are to vote. It is only possible for all electors to have experienced democratic socialization in their youth if a country has had free elections without interruption since the end of the First World War. This criterion is met by seven EU countries, and five more have consistently held free elections since 1945.

Political sociologists assume that a country's social and economic features, such as material prosperity and levels of education, will be the primary influences on electoral participation. Factor analysis shows that gross domestic product (GDP) per capita, employment in non-agricultural sectors, education and the foreign population of a country form a single factor, while government expenditure as a percentage of GDP forms a second factor. For clarity, the multitude of socio-economic influences are therefore reduced to one for each factor, in order to test the next hypotheses—that election turnout will be higher if:

- *Citizens are materially better off.* For comparative purposes, material well-being can be measured by GDP per capita, adjusted by purchasing power parity. The difference between the most prosperous and the least prosperous EU countries is less than 2 : 1. In more prosperous countries, citizens are more likely to be urbanized and therefore to find it easier to reach a polling station, and to be better educated, having a greater awareness of parties, candidates and the importance of elections in a democracy.
- *Government is important for citizens' material well-being.* Empirically as well as ideologically, governments differ in the extent to which public expenditure pays for citizens' health care, social security and education. The more a government raises in taxes, the more money it is able to spend on welfare policies benefiting large

segments of the electorate. The combination of higher taxes and greater benefits increases the incentives for individuals to vote, whether to keep benefits high or to cut high taxes. Public expenditure as a percentage of national GDP varies from a low of 29.3 per cent in Ireland to to a high of 55.1 per cent in Sweden.

While each of the above propositions is familiar, they cannot all be true, or at least equally true. The number of elections since 1945 is large enough to produce statistically reliable tests of alternative theories about what makes for differences in turnout. After controlling for the effects of other influences, statistical analysis shows that all five political variables have a significant independent influence on turnout (figure 2.3). Where citizens have lived all their lives in a democratic system, net of other factors turnout is almost 10 percentage points higher than in new democracies such as Spain, Portugal and Greece[2]. Proportional representation also has a considerable impact: its use can raise turnout by 8.8 percentage points net of other influences. Making voting compulsory tends to raise turnout by 5.3 percentage points. Calling elections on a rest day raises turnout by 3.9 percentage points, net of other influences. The number of electors per MP also affects turnout, but not in the way expected: the greater the number of electors an MP represents, the higher the turnout. However, the impact is slight: increasing the ratio by 10,000 electors, net of other influences, adds only two-thirds of 1 per cent to turnout. Socio-economic factors have no significant influence on turnout. The regression analysis shows that, after controlling for the effect of the influences described in the preceding paragraph, a country's GDP per capita has no effect on turnout. Likewise, the amount of money that government raises in taxes and spends on public policies has no effect on turnout. Additional statistical analyses along similar lines to those in figure 2.3 show that the urban–rural division of the labour force does not affect voter turnout, nor does the percentage of foreign migrants.

Elections to the European Parliament
The EU originated as an elite bargain between national leaders concerned with preventing another war in Europe. The 1957 Treaty of Rome was not a response to popular pressures, nor was it subject to national referendums. The expansion of membership has sometimes required referendum votes, some of which have been lost, most notably in Norway. On occasion, two referendums have been held before the electorate produced the result the political elites wanted, for example, in Denmark and in Ireland.

Elections to the European Parliament were first held in 1979, more than two decades after the foundation of what was then the European Economic Community (EEC). Nine countries participated in the founding election. Elections have been held at five-year intervals since then, with additional countries participating as the EU has enlarged. In the first election, turnout averaged 65.9 per cent, a lower figure than national elections around that time. At each election since, participation in European Parliament elections has declined. In 1999 turnout was 52.8 per cent.

There are very great differences between the member states in the proportion of electors participating in elections to the European Parliament (figure 2.4). In Belgium, where voting is compulsory, an average of 91.2

Figure 2.3: Influences on Voter Turnout in the EU Member Countries
Results of a multiple regression analysis explaining 59.1% of the variance in turnout in 233 national elections from 1945 to April 2002

	b[*]	Beta[a]
Length of time over which free elections have been held[b]	4.9	0.44
Proportional representation	8.8	0.43
Compulsory voting	5.3	0.29
Election day a rest day	3.9	0.23
Electors per MP ('000)	0.066	0.22
GDP per capita	not significant	
Government expenditure as a % of GDP	not significant	

[a] The b value is the unstandardized regression coefficient; the Beta value is the standardized regression coefficient.
[b] The lengths of time for which countries have held free elections are divided into three categories: (a) for the lifetime of present-day voters; (b) consistently since 1945; and (c) for about a quarter-century (Greece, Portugal and Spain).

Source: Figures supplied from the International IDEA Voter Turnout database for elections in all EU member countries from 1945 to April 2002.

per cent participate, and in Luxembourg the proportion is almost as high. At the other extreme, less than one-third of British voters participate in a European Parliament election. In five more countries—Sweden, Finland, the Netherlands, Denmark and Portugal—less than half the electorate can be bothered to vote for their representatives at the European level of governance.

Differences between the percentage turning out to vote in national and in European Parliament elections are also striking. In the UK and Sweden, turnout at European Parliament elections averages less than half that at national

Part I: Current Issues in Voter Turnout

Figure 2.4: Turnout in Elections to the European Parliament, by Country, 1979–99

	No. of European Parliament elections	Turnout in European Parliament elections (%)	Turnout in national elections (%)	Difference
Sweden	2	40.2	80.8	– 40.6
United Kingdom	5	32.3	72.1	– 39.8
Denmark	5	49.4	88.3	– 38.9
Netherlands	5	44.3	81.3	– 37.0
Germany	5	58.0	82.9	– 24.9
Austria	2	58.3	80.4	– 22.1
Finland	2	43.8	65.3	– 21.5
Portugal	4	49.9	66.1	– 16.2
Ireland	5	54.8	70.9	– 16.1
France	5	53.1	68.9	– 15.8
Spain	4	61.7	73.5	– 11.8
Italy	5	79.0	86.6	– 7.6
Greece	4	74.7	81.5	– 6.8
Belgium	5	91.2	92.7	– 1.5
Luxembourg	5	87.9	87.9	0

Note: Turnout is the average for all elections held since the country's first European Parliament election.

Source: Figures supplied from the International IDEA Voter Turnout database.

Figure 2.5: Influences on Turnout in Elections to the European Parliament, 1979–99 (UK 1979–1994)

Results of a multiple regression analysis explaining 65.4% of the variance in turnout in 63 national European Parliament elections, 1979–99.

	b	Beta[a]
Compulsory voting	22.6	0.50
Proportional representation	13.0	0.29
Election day a rest day	10.5	0.27
Duration of EU membership (years)[b]	5.0	0.27
Govt. expenditure as % of GDP	– 0.6	– 0.21
Electors per MP ('000)	not significant	
GDP per capita	not significant	

[a] The b value is the unstandardized regression coefficient; the Beta value is the standardized regression coefficient.

[b] Four categories of duration of EU membership are used: (a) the six founder countries; (b) three older members, the UK, Ireland and Denmark; (c) three newer members, Spain, Portugal and Greece; and (d) the three newest members, Sweden, Finland and Austria.

Source: Figures supplied from the International IDEA Voter Turnout database.

parliamentary elections. In Denmark and the Netherlands the gap between the two types of election is similarly vast. On average, the gap between turnout in European Parliament elections and national elections held in the same period is 18.8 percentage points. Luxembourg is the one country that has found a way of making turnout the same: it holds its national election on the same day as the European Parliament election. However, no other European government wants to tie its hands thus, nor is there likely to be popular acceptance of allowing a five-year gap between one national election and the next in order to ensure that national elections fall on the same day as elections to the European Parliament.

As in national elections, electoral arrangements are the major influences on turnout in European Parliament contests. A multiple regression statistical analysis of turnout in elections to the European Parliament shows that the most important influence, compulsory voting, raises turnout by 22.6 per cent net of other influences. PR is second in impact, raising turnout by 13.0 per cent, and making election day a day of rest also has a double-digit impact on turnout. Habitual socialization is again important, as turnout is higher in countries that have been longest in the EU. Net of other influences, government expenditure as a percentage of GDP has a limited impact on turnout, with voting lower in high-spending countries. Per capita GDP is insignificant as an influence on whether people vote.

Voter Turnout in Western Europe

Political Participation as an Issue

The level of participation in elections is much higher than the proportion of the population who watch current affairs programmes on television, read newspapers which report political events in detail or are well informed about politics. Moreover, the exigencies of government require most political decisions to be taken by representative assemblies or by executive officials accountable to the parliament.

Voting is the one political activity in which a majority of adults participate. Yet turnout falls short of 100 per cent. Democratic idealists claim that everyone ought to participate in elections because it is a civic obligation. Moreover, 100 per cent participation would avoid the risk of representative assemblies not representing the whole spectrum of public opinion in a country. However, the means most suitable to approach this ideal—compulsory voting—is challenged by libertarians who emphasize that in a free society everyone has the right *not* to vote if they so choose. Only totalitarian regimes such as the Soviet Union have compelled citizens to participate in political activities.

Ironically, even where countries have or have had compulsory voting, turnout falls short of 100 per cent. For example, in the Netherlands in the 1950s an average of 5 per cent of the registered electorate did not cast a vote. In Belgium, where voting is still compulsory, almost 10 per cent of the registered electorate does not vote. Libertarian values have gained strength throughout Western Europe, and the Dutch and Austrian parliaments have repealed compulsory voting laws (see also chapter 3). In societies in which the politically indifferent have not been socialized into a sense of the civic obligation to vote, introducing compulsory voting is likely to be less successful because it conflicts with libertarian and laissez-faire norms. It would create very substantial problems of imposing effective penalties and could even be counterproductive if each election produced massive evidence of 'scoff law' non-voters going unpunished—or, if forced to vote, registering support for extremist parties or frivolous parties of Beer Drinkers or the Right Not To Vote.

While compulsion is politically unpopular today, national parliaments can take measures to encourage non-voters to come to the polls. Holding elections on a day when the great majority of the population is not working does increase turnout. In a secular era when people can usually do what they want on the Sabbath, religious objections to Sunday voting carry little weight. There are a number of EU member countries where changing an election date from a weekday to the weekend would produce little opposition.

Making it easier for individuals to cast an absentee vote can, in principle, increase turnout. This can be done in various ways, for example, allowing people to vote by post, in person at a different polling station than that for their normal home address, or by email or telephone. But each of these measures requires safeguards against fraud. If postal votes are mailed out but there is no means of verifying the identity of the persons who use them, they can be cast by 'ghost' voters. If people vote away from home, they must have a positive means of identification, which does not exist in the UK, where there is principled opposition to requiring every citizen to have a national identity card. An email or telephone vote invites impersonation and subsequent controversy when people find that their names have been falsely invoked by an unknown caller from a pay phone or an Internet café. The introduction of safeguards, such as registering a password for an email vote, would reduce the risk of fraud but would also make absentee voting more difficult.

Arguably, declining electoral turnout is a rational response of citizens to the fact that elections make less difference to the way in which a country is governed, as party competition no longer reflects a *kulturkampf* or class conflict, and parties that are nominally on the left and the right have tended to converge towards the centre in pursuit of votes. Moreover, when the government is accountable to a parliament that is elected by proportional representation, elections may determine the relative strength of parties in parliament but it is inter-party bargaining between political elites that determines who actually governs.

Although elections may be declining in popular concern, the impact of government on the lives of citizens has been steadily rising, as is shown by the growth in public expenditure to two-fifths or more of GDP across the EU as a whole. The money collected is not burned but spent on public services such as education, health care, social security, roads and rubbish collection. The average European household regularly enjoys at least two such benefits. In addition, citizens look to government to prevent unsafe vehicles from being driven on the road, to protect them against bank and commercial fraud and against impure food, and much more.

The growth of government has led to the growth of single-issue non-governmental organizations (NGOs). Some, such as the anti-abortion 'right to life' campaigners and those wanting to give more aid to Third World countries, advocate a moral cause. Others, such as trade unions and business associations, exist to promote material interests. Individual membership of NGOs is invariably a small or even infinitesimal percentage of the national electorate. A 'mass' demonstration of 25,000 people appears big on a television screen, but will constitute far less than 1 per cent of a European country's electorate. The percentage of citizens who are active in NGOs may be no more than the minority who were privileged to vote in elections when the right to vote was undemocratically restrictive. Yet the 'failure' of the majority to participate in mass demonstrations and counter-demonstrations does not annul the right of people to become active in NGOs lobbying government.

Corporatism, by which business, labour, agricultural and professional organizations bargain, provides virtual representation of individuals. But corporatist NGOs consist of organizations rather than individuals. For example, business associations are made up of firms and 'peak' associations such as the British Trades Union Congress have other organizations as their members. In Brussels, where thousands of organizations advocate causes to the EU, the typical NGO consists of the aggregation of national NGOs—a further remove from individual participation.

Problems of representation are even greater at the level of the United Nations, since the principle of 'one country, one vote' gives equal representation to countries such as India and Iceland, even though there is more than a thousandfold difference in population between them. At the International Monetary Fund, representation is not based on national sovereignty on an equal basis or weighted by population but determined by the amount of money that countries contribute to the fund.

Elections remain important because they are an effective way of giving those who govern a country incentives to take popular interests into account by the sanction of removing from office governors who fail to do so. But elections are not all-important, for the complexity of interest articulation and aggregation in the multi-level world of local, national, European and global politics imposes constraints on what popularly elected governments can do. Similarly, the existence of competing values—civic participation, individual liberty, facilitating voting, and protecting against fraud—places constraints on what can be done to increase turnout at national elections.

Endnotes

[1] In these eight countries there is a statistically significant downward trend in a least squares regression line of turnout over the period within a country and the variance in turnout explained (R^2) by the passage of time is greater than 25 per cent. However, the 'fit' varies substantially between an R^2 of 95 per cent in Portugal and 28 per cent in the UK. Moreover, the trend fall in turnout from one election to another varies too. In Portugal there is a trend fall of 3.1 per cent in turnout from one election to the next while in Ireland there is a trend decrease of only 0.43 per cent between elections.

[2] The calculation of impact makes use of the unstandardized coefficients (b values) reported in figure 2.3, which are for either/or variables for proportional representation, compulsory voting and rest day; a tripartite classification, as explained in the note to figure 2.5, for duration of democracy; and a continuous variable for number of electors per representative.

References and Further Reading

Blais, André and Dobrzynska, Agnieszka, 'Turnout in Electoral Democracies', *European Journal of Political Research,* 33/2 (1998), pp. 239–61

Franklin, Mark N., 'The Dynamic of Electoral Participation', in Lawrence leDuc, Richard G. Niemi and Pippa Norris (eds), *Comparing Democracies 2: New Challenges in the Study of Elections and Voting* (London and Thousand Oaks, Calif.: Sage Publications, 2002), pp. 148–68

Lijphart, Arend, 'Turnout', in Richard Rose (ed.), *International Encyclopedia of Elections* (Washington, DC: CQ Press, 2000), pp. 314–22

– 'Unequal Participation: Democracy's Unresolved Dilemma', *American Political Science Review,* 91/1 (March 1997), pp. 1–14

Rose, Richard, 'Evaluating Election Turnout', in *Voter Turnout from 1945 to 1997: a Global Report on Political Participation* (Stockholm: International IDEA, 1997), pp. 35–46

– Munro, Neil, *Elections and Parties in New European Democracies* (Washington, DC: CQ Press, 2003)

3. Compulsory Voting in Western Europe

Maria Gratschew

Duty, Right or Privilege?

Is voting a citizen's right or a civic obligation? All democratic governments consider voting in national elections a right of citizenship. Some regard voting in elections as a citizen's civic responsibility, perhaps even a duty. In some of those countries where voting is regarded as a duty, it has been made compulsory to vote, and sanctions are imposed on non-voters in several European countries.

European countries were among the first to grant women the right to vote, and several of them were also among the first to introduce compulsory voting. The process of extending the franchise to men had been less controversial in most countries, but in several instances the right to vote was combined with an obligation to participate and vote in elections.

Compulsory voting is not a new concept. Liechtenstein (1922), Belgium (1893), Argentina (1914), Luxembourg (1919) and Australia (1924) were among the first countries in the world to introduce compulsory voting laws. There are also examples of countries that have had compulsory voting at some time in their history but have since abolished it: for instance, Venezuela had compulsory voting until the mid-1990s and in Europe the Netherlands had compulsory voting until 1967. The first election held there without the practice of compulsory voting was that of 1971. Australia is usually brought up as an example of a country that practises compulsory voting. There, the existence and practice of compulsory voting are still controversial. It may come as a surprise to many that currently six countries in Western Europe retain compulsory voting laws (Belgium, Cyprus, Greece, Liechtenstein, Luxembourg and Switzerland) and three more (Austria, Italy and the Netherlands) had such laws in the past but have since abolished compulsory voting or are in the process of doing so. However, only a few of the countries in Western Europe enforce this obligation in practice.

Impact on Voter Turnout

Approximately 30 countries in the world today have regulations that make voting compulsory in their constitutions or electoral laws. Most of them are in Latin America or Western Europe, but there are a few examples from Asia as well (e.g. Thailand and Singapore). However, any figure for the exact number of countries that practise compulsory voting would be misleading. The simple presence or absence of compulsory voting laws in itself is far too simplistic a measure. It is more constructive to analyse compulsory voting as a spectrum, ranging from the existence of a symbolic but basically impotent law to a system that systematically follows up each and every non-voting citizen and implements sanctions against them.

From the perspective of a voter, if voting is compulsory and sanctions are imposed on non-voters, the rational decision is to vote in elections in order to avoid sanctions. With this reasoning in mind, it comes as no surprise that turnout is usually higher in countries where compulsory voting is practised and enforced. Comparisons of the impact compulsory voting has on turnout show that it is approximately 10–15 per cent higher in countries that have compulsory voting and enforce it (Gratschew and López Pintor 2002: 108, 110).

This spectrum reflects the fact that some countries have compulsory voting laws but do not, and have no intention to, enforce them. There are a variety of reasons for this. Not all laws are created to be enforced. Some are passed merely to state the government's position regarding what the citizen's responsibility should be. Compulsory voting laws that do not include sanctions may fall into this category. In fact the law may have some effect on the citizens, even if a government may not enforce it or even have formal sanctions in law for failure to vote. For example, in Austria voting was compulsory in two regions until recently, and sanctions were only weakly enforced, but these regions had a higher average turnout than the national average.

Other possible reasons for not enforcing the laws could be their complexity and the resources needed to enforce them. Countries with limited budgets may not make the enforcement of compulsory voting laws a high priority but still hope that the existence of the law will encourage citizens to participate. The cost of enforcement may lead some electoral administrations to lower their standards of enforcement.

An examination of the best ways of estimating the level of enforcement of compulsory voting laws and sanctions in a country is relevant here. What information is needed in order to measure whether enforcement is strict or relaxed? Information privided by election (or other) authorities might reflect the intentions but not necessarily the situation in practice. The number of cases of failure to vote that have been followed up after an election or the number of cases taken to court would presumably be the best measures to use. Unless all or at least nearly all cases of failure to vote are followed up after an election, the system can hardly be deemed to be one of strict enforcement.

Can a country be considered to practise compulsory voting if the compulsory voting laws are ignored and irrelevant to the voting habits of the electorate? Is a country practising compulsory voting if there are no penalties for not voting? What if there are penalties for failing to vote but they are never or hardly ever enforced? Or if the penalty is negligible? Many countries offer loopholes, intentionally and otherwise, which allow non-voters to go unpunished. For example, in some countries only registered voters are required to vote but it is not compulsory to register. People might then have incentives not to register.

The diverse forms compulsory voting has taken in different countries suggest that our perception of it should be refocused away from assessing it as a practice that is either present or absent and towards studying the degree to which and the manner in which the government forces its citizens to participate.

Figure 3.1 shows a ranking list of average voter turnout among the countries included in this report. The first four, at the top of the list, have or have had some element of compulsory voting. These are Belgium, Austria, Italy and Luxembourg. The Netherlands, which had compulsory voting until 1967, comes seventh on this ranking list. Switzerland, where only one canton out of 26 practises compulsory voting, is at the very bottom of the list. The country has attracted some attention because of its low turnout and frequent referendums; however, in the canton of Schaffhausen, where compulsory voting is practised, turnout is higher than in other cantons. The two most recent parliamentary elections in Switzerland, in 1999 and 2003, show a much higher voter turnout in Schaffhausen than in the other cantons, and average

Voter Turnout in Western Europe

Figure 3.1: Voter Turnout at National Parliamentary Elections in Western Europe and the Practice of Compulsory Voting

Country (no. of elections) since 1945	Votes cast as % of no. of electors registered****	Compulsory voting practised since
Belgium (19)	92.5	1893–
Austria (18)	90.9	1949–1979*
Italy (15)	89.8	1940s**
Luxembourg (12)	89.7	1919–
Iceland (17)	89.5	-
Malta (14)	88.2	-
Netherlands (18)	86.6	1917–1967
Denmark (23)	86.0	-
Sweden (18)	85.7	-
Germany (15)	85.0	-
Western Europe (overall 297)	82.1	
Norway (15)	80.4	-
Greece (16)	79.9	1952–
Spain (8)	75.7	-
Finland (17)	75.6	-
United Kingdom (16)	75.2	-
France (16)	74.8	-
Portugal (11)	73.6	-
Ireland (16)	72.6	-
Switzerland (14)	56.6	-***

* Compulsory voting was practised in the regions of Vorarlberg and Tirol until 2004.

** Sanctions are not enforced.

*** Practised in one canton only, Schaffhausen.

**** This column shows the average turnout at parliamentary elections since 1945.

On the impact of compulsory voting on turnout, see also chapter 2 and figure 2.3.

Source: International IDEA Voter Turnout database.

turnout there is well above the country average. The country average was 43 per cent in 1999 and 45 per cent in 2003, while turnout in Schaffhausen was 62 and 63 per cent in 1999 and 2003, respectively. In one or two other cantons turnout is up to 50–53 per cent, but this is still much lower than in Schaffhausen. A similar pattern can be seen in Austria where the two regions that practiced compulsory voting until recently normally had a higher turnout at elections. Average turnout in the small country of Liechtenstein is also very high and if it were included it would join the four countries at the top of the list in figure 3.1.

For and Against

Advocates of compulsory voting argue that decisions made by democratically elected governments are more legitimate when higher proportions of the population participate. This argument is often adduced in societies where compulsory voting could be particularly effective in making traditionally marginalized groups participate. Advocates of compulsory voting argue further that voting, voluntarily or otherwise, has an educational effect on citizens. Political parties can save money from compulsory voting, since they do not have to spend resources convincing the electorate that it should in general turn out to vote. Finally, if democracy is government by the people—and this presumably includes all the people—then it is every citizen's responsibility to elect his or her representatives.

The leading argument against compulsory voting is that it is not consistent with the freedom associated with democracy. Voting is not an intrinsic obligation and the enforcement of such a law would be an infringement of the citizens' freedom associated with democratic elections.

Part I: Current Issues in Voter Turnout

Austria

Compulsory voting is regulated by federal law in Austria. However, the regions of the country have been able to decide whether they would like this particular part of the law to apply to them or not since 1979. Compulsory voting was introduced with a new law in 1949, and applied to all the regions at that time, although provision for it had been made earlier in the electoral law of 1919 in the region of Vorarlberg and in an article in the electoral law of 1923. Compulsory voting applies to all elections to the regional parliament as well as local elections. After the Second World War it was compulsory to vote in presidential elections. The first election of a president by the people took place in 1951. (Previously the president had been elected by the two chambers of Parliament according to the constitution of the time.)

By the early or mid-1990s all the regions of the country except two, Vorarlberg and Tirol in the extreme west, had abolished compulsory voting. These two regions are set to do so in 2004. While compulsory voting remained, non-voters had the opportunity to explain their abstention–most often the explanation was accepted. If it was not, fines could be applied as a penalty for not voting. The fines were fairly high but in practice usually lower than what the law specifies. The law provided for fines of up to 700 EUR (c. 768 USD as of 10 September 2003) but in practice the amount imposed was usually less than 50 EUR (c. 55 USD as of 10 September 2003). The provisions for compulsory voting was made in the regional laws of Vorarlberg and Tirol.

Belgium

Belgium was one of the first countries in the world to introduce compulsory voting on the national level. This happened in 1893, long before universal suffrage was introduced. Compulsory voting was introduced to avoid upper-class citizens putting pressure on uneducated or poor citizens not to vote in the elections. It applies to all elections, national and municipal as well as elections for the European Parliament. A non-voter has the opportunity to explain his or her abstention and if the reason for not voting is accepted the case is not taken any further. If it is not accepted the non-voter faces a fine of 5–10 EUR for the first offence (c. 5–10 USD as of 10 September 2003). The fine for a second offence is higher, between 10 and 25 EUR, and if a voter fails to vote four or more times within a period of 15 years he or she is excluded from the electoral register and disenfranchised for ten years. If the non-voter is a civil servant, another sanction applies as well: he or she is disqualified from promotion.

Cyprus

Voting has been compulsory in Cyprus since 1959, according to the Electoral Law of that year. Voting is compulsory at parliamentary and presidential elections and elections to teh local authorities and the European Parliament, for all voters over the age of 18. Non-voters have the opportunity to explain the reasons why they did not vote in the election before a decision on possible sanctions is taken and do not face sanctions if the rasons are judged to be valid. If they are not, the non-voter will face sanctions in the form of fines. The fine imposed by the court may not exceed 500 CYP (c. 931 USD)as of 10 September 2003.

Greece

Compulsory voting was introduced in the Greek Constitution for the first time in 1952, although it was not introduced by specific wording until 1975. The initiative came from the political parties of the time and was intended to prevent voters abstaining and enhance in practice the principle of universal suffrage. Compulsory voting applies to all elections in Greece, including elections to the European Parliament. Voters above the age of 70 and those who are not mobile because of infirmity are exempted, as are those who are more than 200 km from their assigned polling station on election day. A non-voter has the opportunity to explain his/her abstention, but if the reason given is not accepted by the authorities he or she can face quite severe sanctions, such as imprisonment for up to one month, under the present legislation. Under the old electoral law, which is no longer in force, one possible sanction against non-voters involved restrictions on obtaining a passport or driver's licence. In practice today, however, the compulsory voting rules are of a mainly symbolic character and sanctions are not often applied against non-voters.

Italy

Immediately after the Second World War a new electoral system and electoral law were introduced. Compulsory voting was introduced as part of this electoral law and remained in the electoral law for almost 50 years. Fascism had collapsed and a referendum was called to choose whether Italy should be a monarchy or republic. The monarchists had argued strongly in favour of the introduction of compulsory voting and hoped to win the referendum by ensuring broad participation. It was compulsory to vote at all elections. The sanctions that applied were similar to those applied in Belgium today, that is, a voter who had abstained for several consecutive elections would be temporarily suspended from voting. In addition, the sanctions involved a non-voter being unable to obtain employment as a civil servant or run for any public office. Voter turnout has been quite high throughout the years in Italy and sanctions have seldom been imposed on the small proportion of voters who abstained from voting, despite the provision for sanctions in the law. Compulsory voting has been a controversial issue for many years. Those who have argued against it have been mainly the liberal parties. Finally, in the early 1990s, with the country having had more than 55 governments in less than 50 years, all political forces agreed on the need for major reforms in the electoral law.

Voter Turnout in Western Europe

A new electoral law was introduced in 1993 after being accepted by a national referendum. At present the law says that voting is a right and a duty, without using the word 'compulsory'.

Liechtenstein

Liechtenstein introduced compulsory voting early. It has been practised continuously since 1922 and is an integral part of the electoral law of the same year. According to the Government Chancellery it was practised even earlier, possibly as early as 1862, and according to popular memory it has 'always' been the tradition. During the 19th century, the law only applied to men above the age of 24. (Interestingly, as a contrast, Liechtenstein was among the last countries in the world to grant women the right to vote: this was done as late as 1984. Those who stayed away from voting without giving an approved reason were liable to a fine of 1 Guilder, which for some might have been a large sum of money at the time. Even in the 1950s and 1960s the municipality police imposed fines on those who had failed to vote, but this old tradition slowly died out once local councils realized that the cost of enforcing this law exceeded total receipts from the fines. The present law that regulates compulsory voting is from 1973. Compulsory voting applies to all elections and referendums in Liechtenstein. Non-voters may be fined if they have not given an approved reason for not voting. The fine does not exceed CHF 20 (c. USD 14 as of 10 September 2003) and this sanction is rarely enforced in practice.

Luxembourg

A small country, Luxembourg introduced compulsory voting very early, in 1919, and during the same year women were granted the right to vote. Voting is compulsory for elections to the Chamber of Deputies and the European Parliament, and municipal elections. People above the age of 70 and those who are abroad on election day may be exempted from the obligation to vote if they are able to prove this. The electoral law states that a non-voter will be punished by fines on the first occasion he/she fails to vote. Following a second offence, if it is within six years of the first, a larger fine is imposed. The fines range from 99 to 991 EUR (c. 108–1087 USD as of 10 September 2003). In practice, a non-voter usually only receives a warning after the first offence, but if it is repeated the case may be taken to court for further decision.

The Netherlands

With the constitutional change in 1917 which also introduced universal suffrage (for men; women were granted the right to vote in 1919) and proportional representation (PR), compulsory voting was introduced. There were two main reasons for introducing it: (a) the act of voting is a task that serves the public interest and not one's personal interest, and a public right was regarded a public duty in this context; and (b) the newly introduced PR system required a 100 per cent turnout for the election results to be truly proportional. It is worth mentioning that the term 'compulsory voting' was not at first used in the Netherlands, but 'compulsory turnout' was. Compulsory voting applied to all elections. While it existed in the Netherlands, however, it was a much-debated issue and was amended many times.

In 1945 an opportunity to abolish compulsory voting occurred when there was a vote in Parliament on the practice. The groups in favour of keeping it won by one vote, and it was not abolished until 1967 after recommendations made by a committee appointed by the government. A number of theoretical as well as practical arguments were put forward by the committee: for example, the right to vote is each citizen's individual right which he or she should be free to exercise or not; it is difficult to enforce sanctions against non-voters effectively; and party politics might be livelier if the parties had to attract the voters' attention, so that voter turnout would therefore reflect actual participation and interest in politics. The parliamentary election of 1971 was the first to be held without compulsory voting since its introduction.

Switzerland

Compulsory voting is practised in only one out of 26 cantons—the German-speaking northern canton of Schaffhausen, which has practised it for almost 100 years, since 1904. Compulsory voting applied to all elections. The sanction for failure to vote is the same today as it was when the law on compulsory voting was introduced—a fine of 3 CHF (c. 2 USD as of 10 September 2003), which was perhaps a considerable amount 100 years ago but today represents a fairly small share of an average Swiss salary. Other cantons, such as Zürich and Aargau, have also had compulsory voting in the past. Women were granted the right to vote only in 1971, which means that when compulsory voting was introduced it only applied to male voters. By 1971 compulsory voting had been abolished in all cantons except Schaffhausen.

Part I: Current Issues in Voter Turnout

Figure 3.2: Sanctions for Failure to Vote

Country	Type of sanction
Austria	Explanation by non-voter but thereafter fines (abolished in 2004)
Belgium	Explanation by non-voter, thereafter fines or disenfranchisement
Cyprus	Explanation by the non-voter, thereafter fines
Greece	Explanation by the non-voter, thereafter imprisonment. Earlier other sanctions (see page 28)
Italy	Currently none
Liechtenstein	Explanation by the non-voter, thereafter fines
Luxembourg	Explanation by the non-voter, thereafter warning and/or fines
Netherlands	Currently none
Switzerland	Explanation by the non-voter, thereafter fines

It may discourage the political education of the electorate because people who are forced to participate will react against the perceived coercion. Is a government really more legitimate if the high voter turnout is achieved against the will of the voters? To achieve a high voter turnout by using compulsory voting is perhaps easier than ensuring quality in participation. Opponents of compulsory voting argue that the optimal participation is that which is based on the voters' own will to participate in choosing their representatives. Many countries with limited financial capacity may not be able to justify the cost of maintaining and enforcing compulsory voting laws. It has also been proved that forcing the population to vote results in an increased number of invalid and blank votes compared to countries that have no compulsory voting laws (Puplick and McGuiness 1998).

Another consequence of compulsory voting is the possible high number of 'random votes'. Voters who are voting against their free will may tick off a name at random, particularly the name at the top of the ballot paper. The voter does not care for whom he or she votes as long as the government is satisfied that they have fulfilled their civic duty. What effect does this unmeasurable category of random votes have on the legitimacy of the democratically elected government?

Despite the fact that six countries in Western Europe have compulsory voting today, it seems that the level of enforcement of these laws is lower than it used to be. Figure 3.2 lists all these countries and the sanctions they apply. We already know that two countries, the Netherlands and Italy, have abolished compulsory voting, and several countries have gone from enforcing the compulsory voting laws strictly to not enforcing them very strictly, for example, Greece and Liechtenstein. Is compulsory voting a dying phenomenon in Western Europe? Perhaps in a few years it will only be kept as a 'ghost' in countries' constitutions, without any intention to enforce it. If turnout continues to decline—in Europe in general and at elections to the European Parliament in particular—and if politics alone does not succeed in making voting interesting enough, will the introduction of compulsory voting be considered? Or will more countries in the region adopt the practice on a national level if voter turnouts decline?

In most of the European countries where it is found, compulsory voting was introduced 50 years ago or even earlier, in the political systems of the time. Perhaps it is because of its long history that it is commonly accepted or tolerated in the countries that still practise it today. To introduce it in today's European democracies might be more controversial than practising it where is already exists. One example of the resistance compulsory voting could face is the reaction in Sweden in 1999 when the Minister for Democracy, on being asked a question on the subject, mentioned compulsory voting as a means of increasing turnout or keeping it high (*Svenska dagbladet* 29 July 1999, 9 August 1999; and *Borås tidning* 18 August 1999). It is important to note that, even though the minister did not suggest that compulsory voting should be introduced, but merely referred to the high turnout shown in countries that practise it, the media, political scientists and politicians rejected the idea quickly and in strong terms in a heated debate.

At the present stage it is impossible to tell which direction the phenomenon and practice of compulsory voting will take in Western Europe, since some countries aim to enforce it strictly and others do not, for different reasons of principle—political, economic, social or other.

References and Further Reading

Administration and Cost of Elections (ACE) Project, <http://www.aceproject.org>

Austrian Ministry of Interior, Electoral Office, <http://www.bmi.gv.at>

Belgian Ministry of Interior, <http://www.belgium.be/eportal/imdex.jsp>

Blais, André, Dobrzynska, Agnieszka and Massicotte, Louis, *Why is Turnout Higher in Some Countries than in Others?* (Elections Canada, 2003, <http://www.elections.canada.ca>)

Borås tidning, 18 August 1999, 'Demokratins blodomlopp: i modern forskning om valdeltagandet har man kunnat konstatera att det i stor utsträckning är valens viktighet som bestämmer hur högt valdeltagandet blir' [The circulation of democracy's blood: modern research has shown that the importance of the election largely decides how high voter participation will be]

Cyprus Ministry of Interior, Public Administration and Decentralisation, Directorate General of Development Plans, Department of Elections <http://www.cyprus.gov.cy>

Gratschew, Maria and López Pintor, Rafael, 'Compulsory Voting', in *Voter Turnout from 1945 to Date: A Global Report* (Stockholm: International IDEA, 2002)

Greek Embassy in Sweden, Press Officer, private communications

Greek Ministry of Interior, <http://www.ypes.gr>

Hirczy, Wolfgang, 'The Impact of Mandatory Voting Laws on Turnout: A Quasi-Experimental Approach', *Electoral Studies,* 13 (1994), pp. 64–76

Italian Ministry of the Interior, <http://www.interno.it>

leDuc, Lawrence, Niemi, Richard G. and Norris, Pippa (eds), *Comparing Democracies: Elections and Voting in Global Perspectives* (Thousand Oaks, Calif.: Sage, 1996)

Liechtenstein Government Chancellery, <http://www.liechtenstein.li>

Lijphart, Arend, 'Unequal Participation: Democracy's Unresolved Dilemma', *American Political Science Review,* 91/1 (March 1997)

Luxembourg Chamber of Deputies, <http://www.chd.lu/default.jsp>

Major, Shaun, *To Vote or Not to Vote? Compulsory Voting in Australia* (Western Australian Electoral Commission, 1995)

Netherlands Ministry of Interior and Kingdom Relations, National Election Board, <http://www.minbzk.nl>

Puplick, C. and McGuiness, P., 'The Pros and Cons of Compulsory Voting', *Elections Today,* 7/3 (1998)

Svenska dagbladet, 29 July 1999, 'Låt oss slippa röstplikt' [Let us avoid compulsory voting]

Svenska dagbladet, 9 August 1999, 'Röstplikt är kanske inte så dumt?' [Perhaps compulsory voting isn't such a bad idea?]

Swiss Federal Chancellery, Section of Political Rights, <http://www.admin.ch/ch/d/pore/index>

University of Florence, Department for Political Science and Sociology, <http://www.unifi.it>

# 4. Women and the Vote in Western Europe

Nina Seppälä

- *Did you know that women in Liechtenstein gained the right to vote only in 1984?*
- *Did you know that, as overall turnout is declining in Western Europe, women have become more likely to exercise their right to vote than men?*

The Right to Vote: An 80-Year Battle

European women first achieved the right to vote in 1906 in Finland, a country that was in the process of becoming independent from tsarist Russia. Women participated in the national struggle against the tsar's decision to reverse the autonomous status the country had enjoyed. This movement culminated in a parliamentary reform that extended the universal right to vote to both sexes. Soon after, before the First World War broke out, women were given the right to vote in other Nordic countries, with the exception of Sweden. The right to vote in municipal elections had often preceded the suffrage in parliamentary elections.

Figure 4.1 shows that in many countries female suffrage was achieved in the aftermath of the First World War so that by the end of 1919 women were able to vote in the majority of West European countries. In Germany, two social democratic parties formed the first post-war government and introduced the equal voting right that had been one of the issues on their political agendas. In a number of countries the right to vote was gained in two

Part I: Current Issues in Voter Turnout

Figure 4.1: When Women Gained the Suffrage

Country	The right to vote	The right to stand for election
Finland	1906	1906
Norway	1913	1907
Denmark	1915	1915
Iceland	1915	1915
Austria	1918	1918
Germany	1918	1918
Ireland	1918 (1928*)	1918
United Kingdom	1918 (1928*)	1918
Belgium	1919 (1948*)	1921
Luxembourg	1919	1919
Netherlands	1919	1917
Sweden	1919	1919
Portugal	1931 (1976*)	1931
Spain	1931	1931
France	1944	1944
Italy	1945	1945
Malta	1947	1947
Greece	1952	1952
San Marino	1959	1973
Monaco	1962	1962
Andorra	1970	1973
Switzerland	1971	1971
Liechtenstein	1984	1984

* All restrictions lifted.

Source: <http://www.ipu.org, www.db-decision.de/CoRe>.

stages. Belgium, Ireland and the United Kingdom initially placed restrictions on the women's vote. For example, in the UK the franchise was initially only given to married women, women householders and women university graduates aged 30 years or over.

The next countries to extend the right to vote to women were Portugal and Spain in 1931. A female doctor and a widow, Carolina Beatriz Ângelo, had already voted 20 years earlier in Portugal as the law gave the right to vote to the head of the family without defining the sex of this person. In France, women were given the right to vote in 1944 by decree of General Charles de Gaulle after the Senate had repeatedly blocked proposals aimed at enfranchising French women. Italian women acquired the right to vote in 1945 after the fall of fascism, having participated in the liberation movement.

The last West European countries to grant the vote for women were the micro-states of San Marino, Monaco, Andorra and, finally, Liechtenstein—the latter in 1984. It had taken nearly 80 years for all European women to gain a right to vote. Some of them will soon be celebrating the centenary of women's suffrage, while others have had the vote for less than 20 years.

Gender Differences in Turnout

Only limited information is available on the differences between men and women where voter turnout is concerned because most countries do not break down figures by gender. Only Finland, Germany, Iceland, Norway and Sweden do so. The available data is thus not representative of West European countries as it is mostly provided by small Nordic countries.

The data shows that the levels of turnout between men and women differ, producing a 'gender gap'. The size of the difference varies across time and countries, but, as figure 4.2 shows, more men than women turned out to vote until the 1980s in most of the countries under comparison. However, the difference between men and women has been modest since the 1960s. Overall, the gender gap has shrunk in the post-war era and reversed since the mid-1980s so that more women than men now turn out to vote.

Possible Explanations

Many factors have been offered to explain gender differences in voter turnout. However, some researchers suggest that there is in fact no gender difference when the fact that women are over-represented in groups with lower levels of participation is taken into consideration (Newman and Sheth 1984). Similarly, some argue that focusing on the gender gap prevents us from understanding that it is certain groups of women, as opposed to all women, that account for the gender gap (Greenberg 1998). Nevertheless, national election surveys conducted in 19 countries worldwide show that level of education has a strong impact on the different voting behaviour as between men and women. Women at lower levels of education are considerably less likely to vote than men with the same level of education (Norris 2002). It can therefore be assumed that an improvement in women's educational level during the post-Second World War era is an important factor in explaining why women's turnout has improved. Work and socio-economic status, among other factors, are weaker explanatory factors in explaining differences in voter turnout between men and women (Norris 2002).

The Future and Implications of Women's Higher Turnout

Women in older age groups are less likely to vote than the men of their age. However, the trend is the reverse in younger age groups (Norris 2002). From this it follows that women's turnout can be expected to rise in the

Voter Turnout in Western Europe

Figure 4.2: The Gender Gap* in Voter Turnout

[Chart showing Women/Men gender gap in voter turnout from 1945 to 2001 for Finland, Iceland, Sweden, Norway, and Germany]

* The gender gap is the difference between men and women in voter turnout.

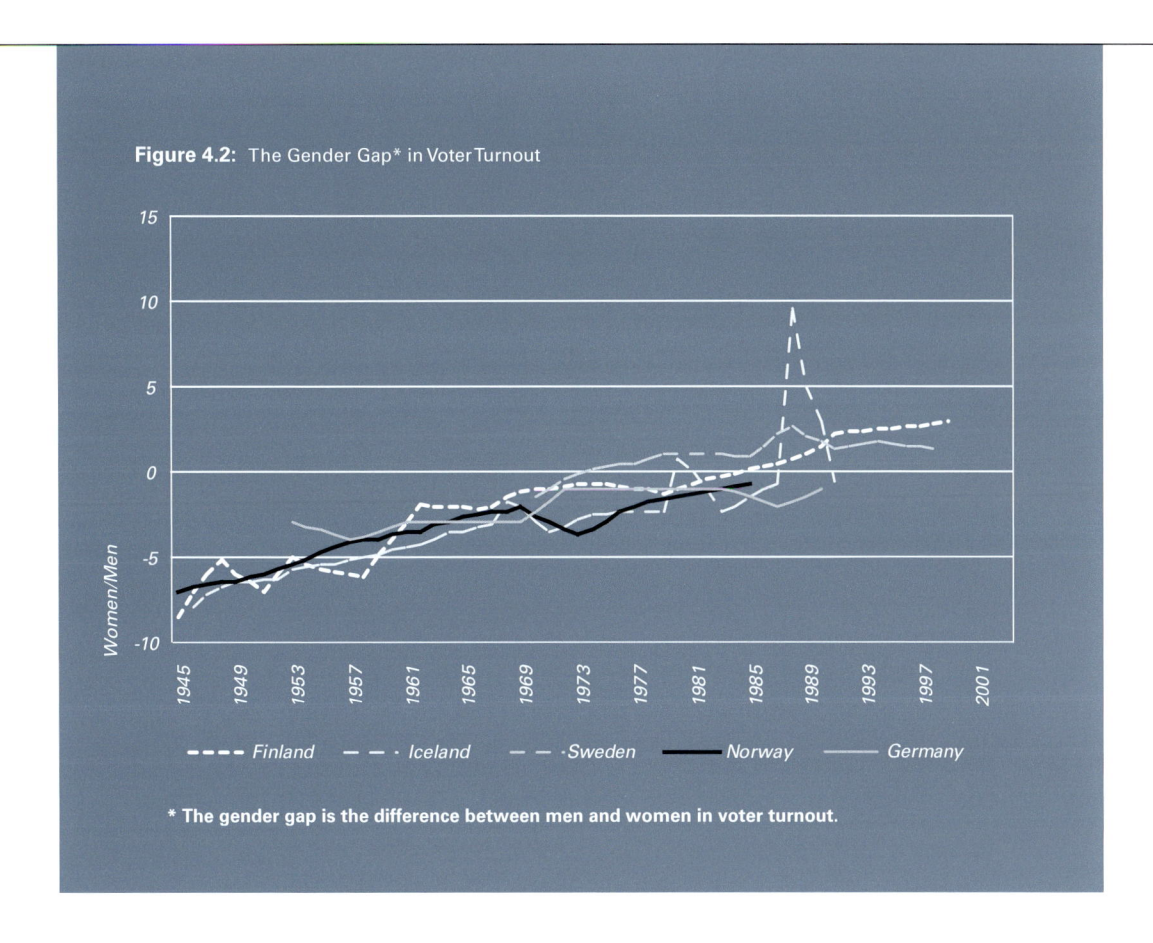

future as well as a younger generation replaces the older.

Some political parties have recognized women as a critical electoral force. For example, in the 1997 British electoral campaign, female voters were targeted by all the major parties (Hayes and McAllister 2001).

Much attention has been paid recently to the question *who* women vote for. Traditionally, women tended to vote more than men for the centre–right (Duverger 1955; and Lipset 1960). By the 1980s this tendency had weakened or reversed in many West European countries. In the Netherlands, Denmark and Italy women had become more left-wing than men, and in other West European countries they have become less conservative than they were (Inglehart and Norris 1999). Women's higher turnout, in conjunction with the trend of weakening support for conservative parties and a leaning towards the left, is having an increasing impact on the political map of Western Europe.

Call for Countries to Disaggregate Turnout Figures by Gender

International IDEA invites electoral authorities to help in collecting voter turnout data that is broken down by gender. This is important for the following reasons:

- to confirm or challenge beliefs about differences in voting behaviour between men and women;
- to provide valuable research data making it possible to identify trends across time and countries; and
- to serve as a basis for the design, targeting and evaluation of campaigns to get people to vote.

References and Further Reading

Duverger, Maurice, *The Political Role of Women* (Paris: UNESCO, 1955)

Greenberg, Anna, 'Deconstructing the Gender Gap', Paper prepared for presentation at the Midwest Political Science Association Annual Meeting, Chicago, Ill., 1998, available at <http://www.ksg.harvard.edu/prg/greenb/gengap.htm>

Hayes, Bernadette and McAllister, Ian, 'Women, Electoral Volatility and Political Outcomes in Britain', *European Journal of Marketing*, 35/9–10 (2001), pp. 971–83

Inglehart, Ronald and Norris, Pippa, 'The Developmental Theory of the Gender Gap: Women and Men's Voting Behaviour in Global Perspective', revised version for the *International Political Science Review*, special issue on Women and Politics, 15 May 1999

Lipset, Seymour Martin, *Political Man: The Social Bases of Politics* (London: Heinemann, 1960)

Newman, Bruce I. and Sheth, Jagdish N., 'The "Gender Gap" in Voter Attitudes and Behaviour: Some Advertising Implications', *Journal of Advertising*, 13/3 (1984), pp. 4–16

Norris, Pippa, 'Women's Power at the Ballot Box', in *Voter Turnout since 1945: A Global Report* (Stockholm: International IDEA, 2002)

5. Innovative Technology and its Impact on Electoral Processes

Tim Bittiger

The application of technology to elections and the complexity of the technology used vary from country to country. They depend on the ability of governments to finance innovations and keep them up to standard given the speed of technological development. While the most complex technology is used in Western countries, countries in transition which have large populations, such as India and Brazil, have been most successful in introducing cost-effective new technologies on an extensive scale.

A wide range of technology has been developed and introduced in elections in recent years. The Administration and Cost of Elections (ACE) Project provides the most comprehensive overview (http://www.aceproject.org).

Only a limited number of technical innovations are currently being used on a wide scale or have the potential to be introduced in coming years. These are:

- *electronic voting/counting systems,* specifically machine-readable (optical scanning) voting/tabulation systems and direct recording electronic (DRE) systems; and
- *remote electronic voting,* for example, via the Internet, text messages or telephone.

Electronic voting/counting has already been introduced in a wide range of elections, while remote electronic voting has so far only been used in some localized experiments and is still being tested.

Part I: Current Issues in Voter Turnout

Electronic Voting and Counting Systems

Only in Brazil and India have electronic voting machines (EVMs) been introduced nationwide. They are partly used in Belgium, Canada, Germany, the Netherlands and the United States. Electronic vote counting is used everywhere in Brazil and Germany; Belgium, Bosnia and Herzegovina, Canada, India, the Netherlands, Norway, Palau, Switzerland, Turkey, the United Kingdom and the United States use it only partly. (For more information see <http://www.aceproject.org>; and <http://www.idea.int>.) In the UK and other Western countries an increasing number of companies, unions and membership organizations have started to introduce electronic voting for their internal elections.

Electronic voting and counting have worked well in practice and have been generally accepted by voters. The Netherlands was among the first countries to introduce an electronic voting system on a national scale, starting in 1974. By the general election in May 2002, 95 per cent of all Dutch local authorities provided electronic voting machines (see the web site of the Netherlands Ministry of the Interior and Kingdom Relations, <http://www.minbzk.nl>).

Brazil has developed the most modern and sophisticated electronic voting system in the world and has proved that it can work in a country of continental size, using low-cost technology. Introduced in 1996, its electronic voting system covered all 110 million voters in 5,656 municipalities for the first time for the October 2002 elections. The majority of the Brazilian public and politicians support the reform. The United Nations Electoral Assistance Division (UNEAD) is currently examining Brazil's electronic voting system to see if it can be applied in other UN member countries (see the web site of the State Electoral Tribunal, <http://www.tse.gov.br>).

India is another country which faces demanding election logistics. This is mainly due to the size of the population, the number of polling stations and polling staff required, and the large number of candidates in first-past-the-post districts. India introduced EVMs in November 1998 and extended their use nation-wide in 2004. In the parliamentary elections in 1999, EVMs were used for over 60 million voters. The difficult October 2002 elections in Jammu and Kashmir were held entirely with EVMs. The Indian Election Commission ensured success through massive training and awareness campaigns. The innovations are an 'unqualified success' and have been well received by parties, candidates and staff, according to the Indian Government. More than 95 per cent of the voters welcomed the use of EVMs in 1999 (Centre for the Study of Developing Societies 1999).

Electronic voting and counting systems have now been tried and tested in a number of countries and it can be argued that the advantages of introducing such technology generally outweigh the disadvantages.

Above all, electronic systems can help to overcome logistical challenges in election processes. They leave elections less vulnerable to poor management and ensure correct reporting of the results and prompt returns. This is especially true for countries that are geographically large and have a large voting population. Brazil and India have shown that it is possible to use new technology on a large scale to process election results very fast. In the October 2002 elections in Brazil, some 360,000 kiosk-style electronic machines were operated by 2 million staff, who tallied the results electronically within minutes after the polls closed. Data was transferred on secure diskettes or via satellite telephone to central tallying stations. These in turn transmitted data electronically over secure lines to tabulating machines in the capital, Brasilia, where the results were calculated within hours. During the same elections, only 1 per cent of polling stations had problems with the new technology.

In the United States, recent studies such as the Caltech-MIT Voting Technology Project found that optical scanning had yielded the best results in US elections between 1989 and 2000. The project recommends that the US states replace punch cards, lever machines and older electronic machines with optical scanned ballot systems and tested electronic voting systems (California Institute of Technology and Massachusetts Institute of Technology 2001).

Electronic systems also serve the voter by making the polling process easier and more transparent because they have a number of user-friendly features. In Brazil, for example, the system displays each candidate's photograph, gives voters the possibility to cast their vote in an electoral district other than the assigned one, and is easy for illiterate and visually impaired voters to use.

This said, there is a discussion about the security of electronic voting and counting systems. Critics of the recent Brazilian elections have pointed out the risks for data storage. They argue that machines can fail to produce results at the end of the day and that the fully digitized system is lacking a back-up in the shape of physical records. However, the experiences of most countries have shown that data storage is usually reliable and accurate.

Some doubt also remains about the scope for controlling and protecting electronic systems against fraud. The Caltech-MIT report warns about risks such as a loss of openness, the presence of 'many eyes' observing, the risk that control over an automated process can be abused, the lack of true auditability, and the lack of public control, but it goes on to say that there are technical solutions for such problems.

There could also be negative implications if an electronic system is not used throughout a whole country or a whole electoral area, or if it is not standardized. In the Netherlands, including Amsterdam, the largest city, some municipalities have not been able to find sufficient funds to automate their elections. This has the effect that results for some electoral districts come in later than others'. Some experts suggest that reform of election technology in the United States can only be successful if state legislation is standardized nationwide, allowing a more streamlined voting system.

Remote Electronic Voting
Remote electronic voting could be the next major innovation in the electoral process but is still in the test phase. This includes voting via the Internet, text messaging (SMS) and the telephone. There is considerable discussion about how to guarantee system security.

A number of research projects are analysing these issues, including:

- *True-Vote,* which is testing public key cryptography as a security feature (<http://www.true-vote.net/HTML/project.html>);
- *CyberVote,* which is analysing Internet voting via personal and palm computers and mobile telephones (<http://www.eucybervote.org>);
- *E-Poll,* which is examining the legal and security issues of e-voting (<http://www.e-poll-project.net/objectives>); and
- *the RTD* (Framework Programme for Research and Technological Development and Demonstration) Project, which is managed by the Information Society Directorate-General of the European Commission and is currently testing web-based voting systems for large-scale elections (<http://www.sics.se/arc/evote.html>).

Some countries are already testing remote electronic voting in official elections, including elections for trade unions and other public institutions. Germany aims to introduce Internet voting in 2006 but live tests have already been launched by the University of Osnabrück, where the official election to the student parliament in 2000 was conducted entirely over the Internet (see the project overview at <http://www.internetwahlen.de>).

The United Kingdom implemented the most diverse tests of a wide range of new technologies in electoral pilot schemes at the local elections held in England on 2 May 2002. Several innovations were tested in 30 municipalities. They aimed at increasing voter participation, introducing new voting methods, improving the efficiency of vote counting and providing better voter information.

The technologies included remote electronic voting from any computer, voting via touch-screen kiosks or personal computers in polling stations or other public areas such as libraries and shopping centres, and voting using the Internet, text messaging or the telephone (see the web site of the UK Electoral Commission, <http://www.electoralcommission.gov.uk>; and chapter 6).

Another set of substantial tests for remote electronic voting is under way in the Netherlands where the government is conducting a Remote E-voting Project aimed at giving voters several options in order to make voting less dependent on particular locations. The project aims to test and develop digital technology such as electronic identity cards in the June 2004 elections, which would allow voters to vote anywhere in their municipality (for details, see <http://www.minbzb.nl>, and the pre-assessment report by the University of Twente—Arts, Leenes and Svensson 2001).

Switzerland launched an experiment in Geneva, Neuchatel and Zurich in 2001 (see the project overview at http://www.admin.ch/ch/d/egov/ve/index.html) Australia, Canada, Estonia, Iceland, New Zealand and Romania are considering remote electronic voting as an option in all or some of their elections but not all have made concrete plans (Arts, Leenes and Svensson 2001).

There is a substantial debate about the feasibility of Internet voting. Most experts argue that its introduction will greatly facilitate polling and that its adoption is a matter of course in the face of current technological developments and voter expectations. The UK Electoral Commission reports that the technical innovations in the May 2002 elections were well received by voters, who found electronic voting 'easy, convenient and quick to use' (UK Electoral Commission 2002). The project also had support from election staff and candidates. However, there are serious questions about the security of such a system, and a great deal of research is centring on this issue. The Caltech-MIT report argues that Internet voting 'poses serious security risks' because individuals such as hackers are able to interfere in election processes, with serious implications (California Institute of Technology and Massachusetts Institute of Technology 2001).

Some experts believe that security issues are more a perceived than a real threat and recommend that public confidence be built actively. The True-Vote project named trust in the Internet as the main problem with remote electronic voting, particularly confidence in the protection of personal information and assurance of the identity of the party the voter deals with during the online transaction. Similarly, the UK Electoral Commission argues that for electronic voting in general 'the central issue is not security per se, but voter confidence'. Although the commission has not observed any negative public concern about the possibility of fraud could reduce trust in the process, and argues that it is necessary to develop technical criteria and inform voters in order to provide reassurance. It holds that a remote electronic system could even increase the security of elections (e.g. through voter identification) and enhance accessibility (e.g. by providing online voter information in minority languages).

Suppliers of New Innovations
A number of private firms are involved in inventing, developing, manufacturing, marketing and maintaining voting equipment and election supplies. Most are based in the United States and the UK, and to a lesser extent in Australia, Canada and the European Union countries.

There are several web-based resources with information on vendors and their services. The most comprehensive is the International Foundation for Election Systems' *IFES Buyer's Guide* (<http://www.ifesbuyersguide.org>), which provides up-to-date and impartial information on market developments. The Centre for Voting and Democracy publishes a citizen's guide to voting equipment, including information and analyses (<http://www.fairvote.org>).

Further developments in 2004:
- In the beginning of 2004, a report was issued on an Internet-based voting system being built for the U.S. Department of Defense's Federal Voting Assistance Program. The report led to an international discussion about security issues of e-voting systems, and is available on http://servesecurityreport.org
- In March 2004, small-scale, non-legally binding electronic voting trials were successfully conducted during the Spanish general elections of 14 March 2004.
- In April 2004, the Irish Commission on Electronic Voting adopted an interim report on the secrecy, accuracy and testing of the chosen electronic voting system. As a consequence the electronic voting system was not used in the local and European elections in June. The interim report is available on http://www.cev.ie/htm/report/V02.pdf
- In July 2004, a group of experts of the Council of Europe adopted a draft Recommendation on legal, operational and technical standards for e-voting. The standards, which apply to remote e-voting as well as to non-remote e-voting, were designed to be accepted and applied by governments and industry alike. The draft recommendation is available on http://www.coe.int/democracy.

References and Further Reading
Administration and Cost of Elections (ACE) Project, <http://www.aceproject.org>

Arts, Kees, Leenes, Ronald and Svensson, Jörgen, *Kiezen op Afstand Monitor. Rapport Vooronderzoek* [Remote voting monitor: pre-assessment report] (Enschede: Twente Research Institute for ICT in the Public Sector, 13 February 2001)

Brazilian State Electoral Tribunal, <http://www1.tse.gov.br>

California Institute of Technology and Massachusetts Institute of Technology, Caltech-MIT/Voting Technology Project, *Voting: What Is, What Could Be* (Boston, Mass. and Pasadena, Calif.: California Institute of Technology and Massachusetts Institute of Technology, July 2001)

Centre for the Study of Developing Societies, New Delhi, 1999, available on the web site of the Election Commission of India, <http://www.eci.gov.in>

Centre for Voting and Democracy, *Citizen's Guide to Voting Equipment*, <http://www.fairvote.org>

CyberVote project, <http://www.eucybervote.org>

E-Poll project, <http://www.e-poll-project.net/objectives>

Election Reform Information Project, *Election Reform since November 2001: What's Changed, What Hasn't, and Why* (Washington, DC, October 2002)

Indian Election Commission, 'Schedule for General Election to the Legislative Assembly of Jammu and Kashmir', Press Note no. ECI/PN/32/MCPS/2002, 2 August 2002

Indian Embassy, Washington DC, 'The Use of Electronic Voting Machines during General Elections, 1999', Press Release, 25 June 1999

International Foundation for Election Systems (IFES), *IFES Buyer's Guide,* <http://www.ifesbuyersguide.org>

International IDEA, <http://www.idea.int>

Netherlands Ministry of the Interior and Kingdom Relations, <http://www.minbzk.nl>

RTD project, <http://www.sics.se/cna/projects.html>

True-Vote project, http://www.true-vote.net/HTML/project.html

Forschungsgruppe Internetwahlen (Research Group Internet Voting), 'i-Vote Report: Chancen, Möglichkeiten und Gefahren der Internetwahl' [Opportunities, possibilities and challenges of Internet voting], Osnabrück, 2002, <http://www.internetwahlen.de>

UK Electoral Commission, *Modernising Elections: A Strategic Evaluation of the 2002 Electoral Pilot Schemes* (London, 2002), <http://www.electoralcommission.gov.uk>

6. Will New Technology Boost Turnout? Experiments in e-Voting and All-Postal Voting in British Local Elections

Pippa Norris*

Proponents argue that the use of remote electronic voting (e-voting) could boost electoral participation, particularly among the young. Pilot schemes carried out among over 6 million people in local elections in the UK suggest that these claims should be regarded with considerable scepticism. Remote e-voting only slightly strengthened turnout among the young—the group least interested in participating. By contrast, all-postal voting boosted turnout among older citizens—the group who are least able to get out to polling stations and the most motivated to take advantage of this reform—by an estimated 18 per cent.

As access to the new communication and information technologies has diffused throughout post-industrial societies, the idea of using electronic tools to modernize the administration of elections has been widely debated. The potential benefits are greater efficiency, speed and accuracy (Norris 2001; Norris 2002 (b); and Norris 2004). Perhaps the most important and influential argument concerns the claim that remote electronic voting will make the process more convenient and thereby strengthen electoral turnout and civic engagement, especially for the 'wired' younger generation (Stratford and

---

*Thanks for their help in the preparation of this chapter are due to the UK Electoral Commission and to Ben Marshall, Kate Sullivan and David Maher for generous help in providing the MORI data and for background briefing papers, as well as to the BBC Political Research Department, in particular Giles Edwards, who also provided invaluable research papers.

Stratford 2001; and Borgers 2002). If citizens will not come to the polls, it is argued, why not bring the polls closer to citizens?

Until recently almost no systematic evidence derived from actual elections was available to allow us to examine this issue. Evidence is, however, available from pilot schemes conducted in local government elections in England in 2000 and 2002, and most recently on 1 May 2003. These contests are characteristically low-salience events where only a third of the electorate usually vote. In constituencies that offered all-postal voting facilities (where the electoral authorities automatically send out ballot papers for postal voting to all those on the electoral register during an extended period before election day, and there is no alternative) turnout was about 50 per cent while, in constituencies in which the pilot schemes used remote e-voting combined with traditional polling stations, remote e-voting proved ineffective in improving overall turnout. There are therefore good reasons to be sceptical about claims that electronic technologies can automatically resuscitate electoral participation. Remote e-voting may expand citizen choice, but it proved far less effective in improving turnout than the use of the old-fashioned post.

In its July 2003 report, *The Shape of Elections to Come*, the Electoral Commission in the UK recommended all-postal votes as standard practice for all local elections, with further evaluation before the practice is extended to other types of election (UK Electoral Commission 2003). With regard to e-voting it was more cautious, suggesting that it should continue to be tested, but with the overall aim of using it as a way of providing citizens with more choice of ways of casting their votes rather than of improving turnout.

Electronic voting can be subdivided into two categories:

- remote e-voting—the transmission of a secure and secret official ballot to electoral officials via various electronic information and communication technologies from a site located away from the polling station, whether from home, the workplace or a public access point. It is sometimes taken to mean only voting by the Internet, but here includes the use of many different electronic devices which are capable of transmitting an electronic ballot, including computers, touch-tone terrestrial telephones, cell (mobile) phones, text messaging devices and digital television; and
- on-site electronic voting used within the traditional polling station, exemplified by touch-activated screens, dedicated computer terminals or electronic counting devices.

The Pros and Cons of e-Voting
Its proponents suggest many advantages that may come from implementing e-voting.

- The most important is the added convenience for the voter. Allowing citizens to cast a ballot from home or the workplace could reduce the time and effort required to participate in person at the polling station. It may also help overcome problems of social exclusion, especially for those with limited mobility, such as the elderly, carers confined to the home by dependent relatives, or employees and shift workers with little flexibility in their work hours, as well as for those who are travelling away from home and for overseas residents. The use of remote e-voting can be regarded in many respects as an extension of the use of other familiar and well tested facilities already widely available in many countries, including postal, absentee, overseas or advance voting. (For the best discussion of the administrative arrangements for registration and voting found around the world see the web site of the Administration and Cost of Elections project at <http://www.aceproject.org>. For further detail see Maley 2000; Blais 2000; Massicotte 2000; Blais and Dobrzynska 1998; Lijphart 1997; Jackman and Miller 1995; Jackman 1987; Powell 1986; and Crewe 1981.)
- Both remote and on-site electronic voting could potentially reduce the 'information costs' of participation by providing relevant information at the time people are actually casting their vote, for example, by incorporating an optional web page display of standardized biographies of candidates or providing a briefing synopsis explaining each side of a referendum issue.
- For officials, well designed and effective electronic technologies, either remote or on-site, could potentially improve and streamline the process of electoral administration, by increasing the efficiency, speed and accuracy of recording and counting votes (see e.g. Barber 1998; Rash 1997; Schwartz 1996; Budge 1996; Rheingold 1993; and Arterton 1987).

Against these arguments, sceptics counter that many current limitations—technological, socio-economic and practical—combine to create substantial barriers to the effective implementation of e-voting.

Technological Barriers
Democratic electoral systems must meet certain stringent standards of security, data protection, secrecy, reliability, accuracy, efficiency, integrity and equality, and public confidence in the integrity of the electoral system must be maintained to ensure the legitimacy of the outcome. Electronic votes cast in a general election could be a high-

profile target for malicious publicity-seeking hackers. Various high-profile cases, the recent spate of disruptive viruses and the volume of e-mail 'spam' may have reduced public confidence in the security of the Internet. Critics claim that the technology required to authenticate voters and to ensure the accuracy and integrity of the election system either does not exist at present or is not sufficiently widely available to be assessed. Task forces reviewing the evidence, such as those of the US National Science Foundation and the British Electoral Reform Society, are doubtful about the technological, security and legal issues surrounding e-voting, suggesting that further exploratory pilot studies are required before it is adopted (Internet Policy Institute 2001; and Independent Commission on Alternative Voting Methods 2002).

When remote e-voting has been tried in small-scale pilot studies, the security and technological issues involved in casting even hundreds of votes electronically have often proved problematic. In October 2001, for example, the residents of the Dutch towns of Leidschendam and Voorburg were given the chance to vote via the Internet on the choices for the merged towns' new name. The vote was abandoned when it became obvious that more votes had been cast than there were electors (British Broadcasting Corporation 7 January 2002). The Arizona Democratic primary election of 2000, which also experienced many technical glitches, has been widely quoted, although it remains difficult to assess how far it is possible to generalize from it given the particular circumstances of this unique contest (Gibson 2002; and Solop 2001).

It remains unclear whether the purely administrative problems that currently surround the practical issues of security, secrecy and integrity might eventually be resolved by technological and scientific innovations. Potential problems of voter fraud might be overcome by advances in biometric voice recognition, retina scanning and fingerprint recognition, for example, or by the widespread use of 'smart cards' as identifiers with a computer chip and unique digital certificates.

Social Barriers
Setting aside these important technical and security matters for the moment, another fundamental issue is the problems that could arise if remote e-voting serves to exacerbate existing structural inequalities in electoral participation. In democracies the electoral process should be equally available to every citizen, without discriminating against any particular group. This important principle is widely recognized in the practices of locating traditional polling stations throughout local communities and of translating the instructions for registration and voting

Figure 6.1: Social Profile of the Online Community, European Union Member Countries, 1996–2000

	% online spring 1996	% online spring 2000	Change 1996–2000
Age group			
15–25	9	28	+ 19
26–44	7	28	+ 21
45–64	5	21	+ 16
65+	1	6	+ 5
HH income category			
- -	4	12	+ 8
-	3	15	+ 12
+	5	24	+ 19
++	10	44	+ 34
Age finished education			
Up to 15	1	7	+ 6
16–19 years	4	19	+ 15
20+	9	38	+ 29
Gender			
Men	6	25	+ 19
Women	4	21	+ 17
Occupational status			
Managers	14	44	+ 30
Other white collar	8	29	+ 21
Manual worker	3	15	+ 12
Home worker	2	8	+ 6
Unemployed	3	10	+ 7
Student	13	44	+ 31
All	5	22	+ 17

Note: HH = Head of household.
Sources: Eurobarometer 44.2 (spring 1996) and 53.0 (spring 2000).

into the languages spoken by minority populations. Critics charge that the use of remote e-voting from home or work could violate the principle of equitable access, given the existence of the familiar 'digital divide' between the information 'haves' and the 'have-nots'—between rich and poor, between graduates and those with minimal educational qualifications, and between the younger and older generations (Norris 2001; and Norris 2002 (b), chapter 5). Making remote voting easier for those with access to electronic technologies could further skew participation, and therefore political influence, towards more affluent and wired socio-economic groups. Surveys by Eurobarometer show the European digital divide in 1996: access to online technologies was concentrated among the younger generations, more affluent households, university graduates, managers and white-collar workers, students and, to a lesser extent, men; and by spring 2000 the social profile had not changed much (see figure 6.1). The strongest rise in access had been among the most affluent households, the well educated, and managerial professionals, although use had spread rapidly among the early-middle-aged as well as the youngest age group. In 2000 the digital divide by age, gender, education, income and class remained significant, as did the marked contrasts in Internet access between the countries of Northern and Southern Europe (Eurobarometer spring 1996, spring 2000). Age is very important for turnout, as is discussed later.

This familiar pattern suggests that the digital divide would probably reinforce, or even widen, many of the familiar socio-economic disparities in electoral participation that already exist, including those of social class, education, gender and income. Yet there is one important qualification to this conclusion: remote e-voting could encourage younger people to take advantage of this opportunity.

This argument does not, of course, apply to other forms of remote e-voting from public kiosks at traditional polling stations or in public places such as libraries, town halls, schools and community centres, where principles similar to those that determine the location of traditional polling stations would apply. But it becomes relevant if remote e-voting is available from any home or workplace computer terminal, which is the most radical and exciting application of this principle. Moreover, poor design could discourage some citizens from voting using new technologies, for example, the disabled, those with low literacy skills or the elderly. On the other hand, the real advantages of e-voting are reduced because people would still have to travel to a public location, while the security problems would remain.

Practical Barriers
The theory that we can use to understand electoral participation, developed more fully elsewhere, suggests that the incentives that motivate citizens to vote represent a product of three factors (see also Norris 2002 (b); and Norris 2004):

- the electoral costs involved in registering to vote, sorting out relevant information, deciding how to vote, and then actually casting a ballot;
- electoral choices, determined largely by the range of political parties, candidates and issues listed on the ballot paper; and
- electoral decisiveness, influenced by how far votes cast for each party, candidate or issue are thought to determine the outcome.

Electoral Costs
The theory assumes that rational citizens will be less likely to vote if they face major costs in participating.

This includes registering as electors, becoming informed about the issues, parties and candidates, and finally casting a ballot to express their voting choice. Standard rational choice theories suggest that, all other things being equal, the deterrent of higher costs reduces electoral participation.

Holding elections on a weekend or holiday, or over a series of days, rather than on a workday can reduce costs (Franklin 2004).

Registration procedures are often believed to be an important hurdle. In many countries, including the UK, Sweden and Canada, registration is the responsibility of the government, conducted via a door-to-door canvas or annual census, so most eligible citizens are automatically enrolled to vote. In others, including the United States, France and Brazil, citizens have to apply to register, often well ahead of the election, and complicated procedures and time-consuming or restrictive practices can depress participation levels (Katz 1997, table 13.2).

In this regard, remote e-voting can be seen as essentially similar in principle to other remote voting facilities that are in common use, exemplified by the widely available special arrangements for mobile populations, including the use of mail, proxy, absentee or overseas votes, as well as polling facilities for the elderly and disabled in nursing homes and hospitals.

Electoral Choices
Electoral choices are determined by broader characteristics of the political system, including the options available on the ballot paper (notably the range of parties and candidates) and the policy alternatives listed for referendum issues. In turn, these options can be related to the type of electoral system, the party system, and other basic political institutions such as a parliamentary or presidential system.

Rational voter theories suggest that in general, all other things being equal, the greater the range of choices available on the ballot, the more easily the voter will find an option (a party, candidate or referendum issue) that reflects his or her own viewpoint, preferences and interests, and therefore the stronger the incentive to vote. Remote e-voting is unlikely to have an impact on any of these factors.

Electoral Decisiveness
Electoral decisiveness, meaning the political benefits anticipated from voting in determining the composition of parliament and government, and the public policy agenda, is also important. In elections that are expected to be close, citizens are likely to feel a greater incentive to get to the polls than they do in those where the outcome appears to be a foregone conclusion. Studies in the UK, for example, have found that, since the Second World

War, the smaller the difference between the national shares of the vote for the two major parties, the higher the level of electoral participation (Heath and Taylor 1999). Of course the actual benefits of casting a single vote may, on purely rational grounds, be illusory, because one vote is unlikely to decide the outcome of an election, but this is not to deny the psychological belief that in close elections each vote counts for more than it does in safe contests.

There are trade-offs between electoral choice and electoral decisiveness. Widening the range of choice on the ballot paper may allow citizens to find a closer match to their interests. But if the party system becomes too fragmented with multiple choices, then casting a vote for a smaller party will be even less likely to influence the outcome. Moreover a wider range of choices increases the costs of becoming informed about alternative candidates, parties and issues.

The introduction of remote e-voting from the home or workplace would probably marginally reduce the costs to the elector of casting a vote at a polling station but it would be unlikely to affect other important costs, such as the significant cognitive demands required to sort out the relevant information in deciding how to vote, nor would it influence electoral choices and electoral decisiveness. The Internet as such cannot be regarded as a panacea for all the ills of electoral participation, which are the result of many deep-seated forces. In particular, it cannot affect how far citizens feel that they have a genuine choice that matches their prior preferences and that their vote counts.

Evidence for Evaluating Remote e-Voting
What evidence would allow us to evaluate these issues? Here we can turn to the UK, which has gone further than any other country in testing the impact of a wide variety of remote e-voting technologies during actual elections.

Concern about electoral participation has risen in the UK. The 2001 general election saw turnout plummet, from 71.5 per cent to 59.4 per cent of the electorate—the lowest since 1918. Moreover, this followed historically low levels of turnout at successive local elections from 1998 to 2000 and in the European Parliament elections of 1999 when only 27 per cent of the electorate bothered to vote. (For details, see the tables in Part III.) This pattern is worrying for democracy as the legitimacy of the electoral process, and the mandate of the government, might eventually be undermined. The Labour government has proposed modernizing electoral administration in the attempt to re-engage the electorate. Recent changes enabled by the Representation of the People Acts 2000 and 2001 include universal postal voting (available on request without a reason having to be given), an extension of the traditional polling hours, and more modern methods of voting, including the use of telephone and Internet-based voting.

Innovations in polling places, polling hours and all-postal ballots were tested in 38 pilot schemes used among 3.5 million eligible electors in the May 2000 local elections and 30 more pilot schemes tried among 2.5 million eligible electors in the May 2002 local elections. The Electoral Commission concluded that these generated interesting preliminary results, with significant increases in turnout (particularly from all-postal voting schemes), no significant technical problems of implementation or electoral management, and no evidence of fraud. Following evaluation, the government signalled its desire to use e-voting by the next general election after 2006, and substantial resources were allocated to fund further pilot studies at local government level. Nevertheless many significant questions remained. The commission concluded that the initial conclusions needed to be tested more extensively, especially facilities for remote e-voting using multiple technologies (UK Electoral Commission 2002).

Accordingly a further series of 59 pilot schemes were conducted in the May 2003 local elections. In all 17 of them explored innovative ways of using remote e-voting. For comparison, the Electoral Commission also continued to examine the use of all-postal ballots in over half of the pilot schemes,[1] and in the remaining constituencies the public cast a traditional in-person vote by marking crosses on standard ballot papers in local polling stations. Examples of the May 2003 initiatives included:

- all-postal voting, Internet and telephone voting throughout, and electronic counting;
- voting via the Internet, by telephone and by SNS text messaging;
- all-postal voting, voting by the Internet, telephone and digital television, and electronic counting;
- voting from terminals in local libraries;
- voting via public kiosks, the Internet, telephone and mobile phone text messaging; and
- extended voting hours.

Other pilot schemes used electronic counting, mobile polling stations and extended polling hours.

The political context in May 2003 was a low-key one, with a strong government in Parliament, the news dominated by events in Iraq, and a degree of 'election overload'. Not surprisingly, overall turnout was down 9 per cent in Scotland (from 1999, the inaugural election for the Scottish Parliament), and 8 per cent in Wales. In England, however, despite expectations, turnout was 37 per cent, a rise of 5 per cent from 1999 and of 3 per cent from 2002.

Part I: Current Issues in Voter Turnout

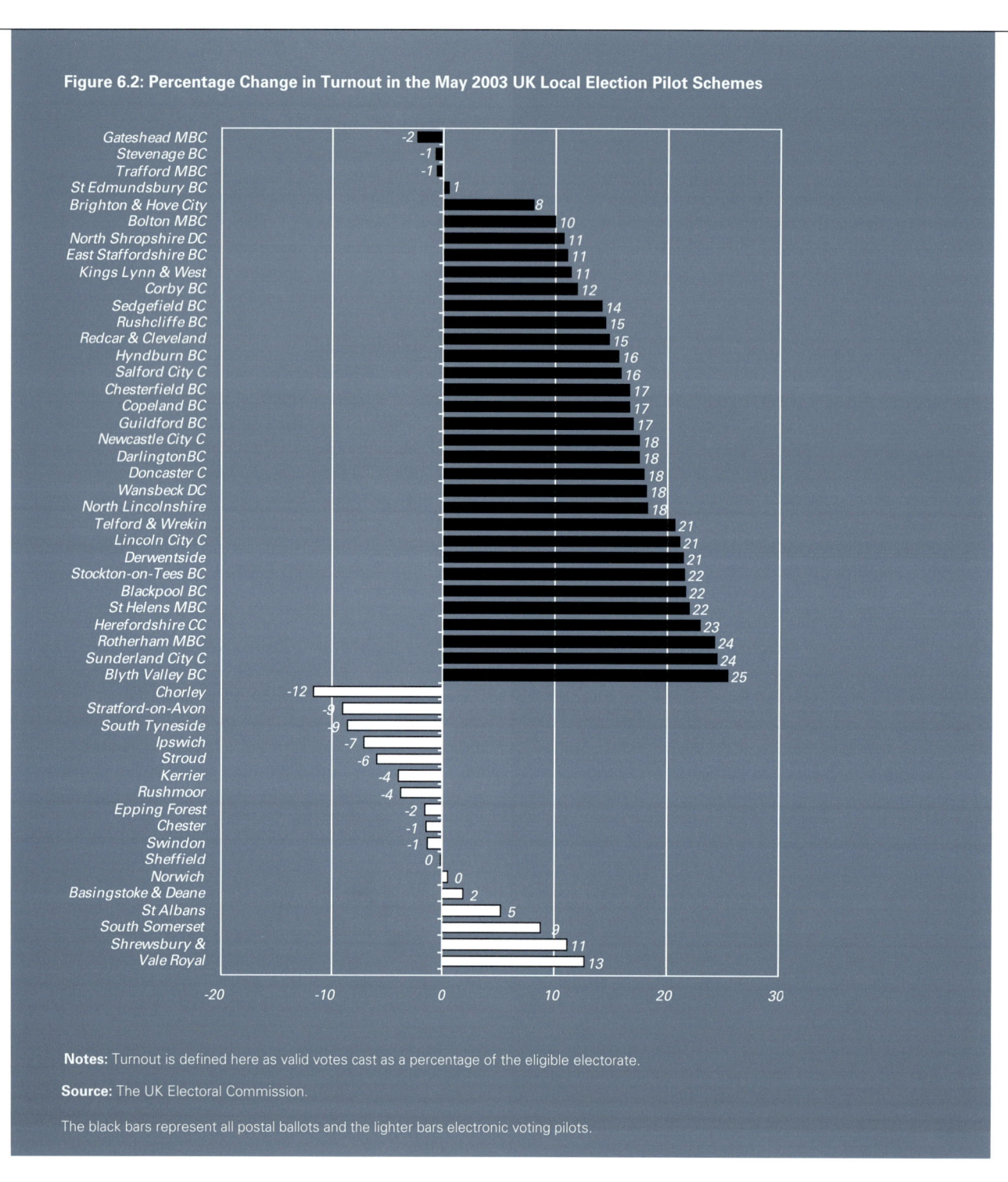

Figure 6.2: Percentage Change in Turnout in the May 2003 UK Local Election Pilot Schemes

Authority	Change
Gateshead MBC	-2
Stevenage BC	-1
Trafford MBC	-1
St Edmundsbury BC	1
Brighton & Hove City	8
Bolton MBC	10
North Shropshire DC	11
East Staffordshire BC	11
Kings Lynn & West	11
Corby BC	12
Sedgefield BC	14
Rushcliffe BC	15
Redcar & Cleveland	15
Hyndburn BC	16
Salford City C	16
Chesterfield BC	17
Copeland BC	17
Guildford BC	17
Newcastle City C	18
Darlington BC	18
Doncaster C	18
Wansbeck DC	18
North Lincolnshire	18
Telford & Wrekin	21
Lincoln City C	21
Derwentside	21
Stockton-on-Tees BC	22
Blackpool BC	22
St Helens MBC	22
Herefordshire CC	23
Rotherham MBC	24
Sunderland City C	24
Blyth Valley BC	25
Chorley	-12
Stratford-on-Avon	-9
South Tyneside	-9
Ipswich	-7
Stroud	-6
Kerrier	-4
Rushmoor	-4
Epping Forest	-2
Chester	-1
Swindon	-1
Sheffield	0
Norwich	0
Basingstoke & Deane	2
St Albans	5
South Somerset	9
Shrewsbury &	11
Vale Royal	13

Notes: Turnout is defined here as valid votes cast as a percentage of the eligible electorate.

Source: The UK Electoral Commission.

The black bars represent all postal ballots and the lighter bars electronic voting pilots.

How far was the increase in the English local elections due to the pilot initiatives?

Two sources of evidence are available to analyse the patterns of turnout. First, we can examine the change in the macro levels of turnout in the local authority districts using the pilot schemes in May 2003 compared against the level of turnout in the last benchmark election in these same areas. Second, to understand the micro-level behaviour of voters and the reasons behind patterns of electoral participation, we can analyse the post-election survey conducted by the opinion poll organization MORI on behalf of the Electoral Commission. MORI interviewed a representative sample of approximately 200 adults aged over 18 years in 29 of the 59 authorities which were piloting new voting arrangements at the May 2003 elections. A total of 6,185 interviews were conducted between 2 and 12 May 2003.[2]

The Impact of e-Voting

In districts where all-postal voting was used, the results illustrate its outstanding success. On average turnout increased from one-third (34 per cent) to almost half (49.3 per cent) of the electorate in these districts. The increase was even more remarkable in some northern areas where turnout had been lowest. Only three saw any slight fall. A 15 per cent average increase in turnout was also found in the 2002 all-postal pilot schemes, and this confirms the consistency and robustness of these results. The Electoral Commission found very limited evidence that the use of all-postal voting led to any increase in fraud or electoral offences. Of course, part of the rise in turnout could be a one-off effect of publicity and novelty value; but the fact that the rise in turnout was fairly substantial and reasonably consistent across many different types of urban and rural areas, as well as different parts of England, suggests that at least some of the benefits of postal voting are likely to persist if it is used more widely in future local elections.

By contrast, the districts using e-voting showed a far more mixed picture of turnout, as illustrated in figure 6.2. Overall only about 9 per cent of the electorate in these districts used the electronic technologies to cast a ballot, with most of the public opting for traditional methods of voting. Three districts using e-voting did experience a rise in turnout of 9–13 per cent, but two of these offered the option of postal voting as well. Overall, two-thirds of the areas experimenting with e-voting registered a modest fall in turnout, disappointing the hopes of the reformers.

All-postal voting and remote e-voting share certain important features. Both offer voters additional convenience over traditional in-person visits to the polling station. So why should areas using these facilities generate such different patterns of macro-level turnout? Here we need to turn to the micro-level survey data to understand more fully how the public responded to these opportunities, and which social groups used the all-postal and e-voting facilities. In particular, even if the electronic facilities generated no positive effects in aggregate turnout that were evident at district level, there could still be differential patterns in which certain social groups took more advantage of the new voting facilities than others. In particular it is important to monitor whether younger people—who are both the most wired generation and also the group least likely to turn out to vote using conventional methods—might prove more likely to vote using e-voting facilities. The MORI post-election survey showed the familiar curvilinear pattern of reported voting by age: as a multitude of studies have found, younger people are persistently less likely to participate, with voting rising to a peak in late middle age, until there is a fall among the over-70s, who often have difficulty in getting out to the polls.

Respondents in the MORI survey can be divided into three major categories according to whether the type of pilot scheme used in their district was (a) combined, (b) any electronic, or (c) all-postal. Figure 6.3 shows the breakdown of reported voting by the type of pilot area and by major age groups.

Figure 6.3: Reported Voting Participation by Age Group in the May 2003 British Local Election Pilot Schemes
Figures are percentages.

Type of pilot	Age group	Did not vote	Reported voting at a polling station	electronically	by post	Total
Combined pilots	Younger	84	N/a	8	8	100
	Middle-aged	61	N/a	9	30	100
	Older	25	N/a	7	68	100
Electronic pilots	Younger	84	10	5	1	100
	Middle-aged	70	20	8	3	100
	Older	47	38	8	8	100
All-postal pilots	Younger	81	N/a	N/a	19	100
	Middle-aged	58	N/a	N/a	42	100
	Older	29	N/a	N/a	71	100

Note: Younger = 18–29 years old; middle-aged = 30–59; older = 60+ years old. N/a = not applicable in pilot area.

Source: MORI post-election survey of 6,185 electors 2–12 May 2003 in 29 local authorities piloting new voting arrangement. The survey results were weighted by wtfinal. For further details see <http://www.mori.com/polls/2003/electoralcommission.shtml>.

In the combined pilot areas there were huge disparities in reported voting participation by age group: 84 per cent of young people said that they did not vote, compared with only one-quarter of the over-60s. Just fewer than one in ten in each of the age groups used the electronic means of voting, and this pattern was fairly similar among young and old. But postal voting proved by far the most popular among the older group, who often have limited mobility.

The all-postal ballot pilots generated similar age differentials to the combined pilot areas: only one-fifth of the younger group reported voting compared with almost three-quarters of the elderly.

The last category of pilot schemes allowed people to cast a ballot either electronically or in the traditional way in person at the polling station. In these areas, electors could also opt for postal vote by application, but did not receive the option automatically. This category saw an intriguing pattern: as we have seen, aggregate levels of turnout actually fell in some of these areas, and overall across all these pilot schemes turnout did not increase. One of the main reasons uncovered by this analysis is that without all-postal voting the elderly are less likely to vote either in person at polling stations or electronically. And in these areas, while younger people do use the new e-voting means, nevertheless they remain less likely to vote than the older generation. Compared with other pilots, the strength of the age regression coefficient is reduced in the electronic pilot schemes, but this effect occurs mainly by depressing the participation of the elderly, rather than by boosting the participation of the young.

Multivariate analysis, introducing controls for gender, race and class into logistic regression models of voting participation in each category of pilot schemes, confirmed that the effect of age remained consistently significant even after applying controls, and that the age effect diminished most under the electronic pilot schemes. This suggests that the use of electronic voting technologies combined with in-person voting in traditional polling stations alone, if not supplemented by the simultaneous use of automatic postal ballots, would not bolster turnout. Quite simply, the older generation remain the least comfortable using new technologies. They are also the social sector with the strongest habit of voting, and yet the least physical mobility, who are therefore most motivated to take advantage of opportunities to cast their ballot by post.

The theory developed earlier suggests that reducing the costs of voting helps, but in order to participate citizens also need to feel that they have genuine electoral choices and that casting a vote will have an important impact through electoral decisiveness. Convenience in casting a ballot therefore only facilitates action if citizens are already motivated by broader political considerations.

Conclusions

The evidence presented in this study suggests that at present, even if the technical and social equality issues could be overcome, there are few grounds to believe that remote e-voting from home or from work on a large scale would radically improve turnout. It would probably have a modest impact on the younger generation, judging by the available evidence from the British pilot studies. And automatic postal ballots are far more effective in improving participation among the older generation, as well as being cheaper and more efficient to administer. Technological quick fixes, while superficially attractive, cannot solve long-term and deep-rooted civic ills. Yet this does not mean that we should abandon all hope of modernizing elections. The impact of all-postal voting proved positive and highly significant.

This is not to argue that the Internet fails to serve many other important functions during election campaigns, including for civic engagement. Content analysis of party web sites suggests that the Internet provides a more level playing field for party competition, serving information and communication functions that are particularly important for minor and fringe parties (Norris 2003). US surveys show that online communities can serve both 'bridging' and 'bonding' functions, strengthening social capital (Norris 2002 (a)). Experimental evidence shows that parties' web sites do indeed promote civic learning, and in this regard information on the Internet is analogous to campaign information from newspapers or television news (Norris and Sanders 2004). But survey evidence from the USA suggests strongly that e-voting would be used primarily by the people who are already most likely to participate, thereby still failing to reach the apathetic and disengaged (Norris 2002 (c)).

Perhaps the main impact of the Internet on democratic life will derive from its ability to strengthen the public sphere by expanding the information resources, channels of electronic communication, and networking capacity for organized interest groups, social movements, non-governmental organizations (NGOs), transnational policy networks, and political parties and candidates (Norris 2001). The debate about remote e-voting may in fact fail to identify the principal impact of the new information and communication technologies on democracy.

Voter Turnout in Western Europe

Endnotes

[1] One evaluation of the experience of all-postal ballots in Oregon found that this had a modest effect on electoral turnout, particularly in low-salience contests, but the main impact was to increase voter participation among the groups already most likely to vote, thereby increasing socio-economic inequalities in turnout (Karp and Banducci, 2000).

[2] There are limitations in what can be analysed using the MORI survey data. In particular, there was no 'control' sample of voters in non-pilot districts. None of the standard attitudinal measures used for analysing turnout, such as political efficacy and partisanship, were used. Many of the questions were filtered so that they were only asked of sub-samples in different pilot areas, thus making comparison across areas impossible. Moreover, the method of classifying 'pensioners' into the DE socio-economic class skewed the age profile in this category, thus making class analysis unreliable. There were also too few representatives of ethnic minorities to allow reliable analysis by racial group.

References and Further Reading

Administration and Cost of Elections (ACE) project, developed by International IDEA and the International Foundation for Election Systems (IFES), <http://www.aceproject.org>

Arterton, Christopher F., *Teledemocracy* (Newbury Park, Calif.: Sage, 1987)

Barber, Benjamin R., 'Three Scenarios for the Future of Technology and Strong Democracy', *Political Science Quarterly*, 113/4 (1998), pp. 573–90

Blais, André, 'Day of Election', in Richard Rose (ed.), *International Encyclopedia of Elections* (Washington, DC: CQ Press, 2000)

— and Dobrzynska, Agnieszka, 'Turnout in Electoral Democracies', *European Journal of Political Research*, 33/2 (1998), pp. 239–61

Borgers, T., 'Is Internet Voting a Good Thing?', *Journal of Institutional and Theoretical Economics*, 156/4 (2002), pp. 531–47

British Broadcasting Corporation (BBC), 'E-voting: A Load of Old Ballots?', 7 January 2002, <http://news.bbc.co.uk/hi/english/in_depth/sci_tech/2000/dot_life/newsid_1746000/1746902.stm>

British Government, Office of the e-Envoy, *In the Service of Democracy*, July 2002, <http://www.edemocracy.gov.uk>

Budge, Ian, *The New Challenge of Direct Democracy* (Oxford: Polity Press, 1996)

Crewe, Ivor, 'Electoral Participation', in Austin Ranney and David Butler (eds), *Democracy at the Polls* (Washington, DC: American Enterprise Institute for Public Policy Research, 1981)

Dictson, Derek and Ray, Dan, 'The Modern Democratic Revolution: An Objective Survey of Internet-Based Elections', 2000, <http://www.Securepoll.com>

Eurobarometer, 44.2 (spring 1996) and 53.0 (spring 2000)

Franklin, Mark N., 'The Dynamic of Electoral Participation', in Lawrence leDuc, Richard G. Niemi and Pippa Norris (eds), *Comparing Democracies 2: New Challenges in the Study of Elections and Voting* (London and Thousand Oaks, Calif.: Sage, 2002)

—*The Dynamics of Voter Turnout in Established Democracies since 1945* (New York: Cambridge University Press, forthcoming 2004)

Gibson, Rachel, 'Elections Online: Assessing Internet Voting in Light of the Arizona Democratic Primary', *Political Science Quarterly*, 116/4 (2002), pp. 561–83

Heath, Anthony and Taylor, Bridget, 'New Sources of Abstention?', in Geoffrey Evans and Pippa Norris (eds), *Critical Elections: British Parties and Voters in Long-term Perspective* (London: Sage, 1999)

Independent Commission on Alternative Voting Methods, *Elections in the 21st Century: From Paper-Ballot to e-Voting* (London: Electoral Reform Society, February 2002), <http://www.electoralreform.org.uk/topstories/elecvoting.htm>

Internet Policy Institute for the National Science Foundation, *Report of the National Workshop on Internet Voting*, Mar. 2001, <http://www.electionline.org/site/docs/html/internet_policy_institute_report_summary.htm>

Jackman, Robert W., 'Political Institutions and Voter Turnout in Industrialized Democracies', *American Political Science Review*, 81 (1987), pp. 405–23

— and Miller, Ross A., 'Voter Turnout in Industrial Democracies during the 1980s', *Comparative Political Studies*, 27 (1995), pp. 467–92

Karp, Jeffrey A. and Banducci, Susan, 'Going Postal: How All-Mail Elections Influence Turnout', *Political Behavior*, 22/3 (2000), pp. 223–39

Katz, Richard S., *Democracy and Elections* (New York: Oxford University Press, 1997)

Lijphart, Arend, 'Unequal Participation: Democracy's Unresolved Dilemma', *American Political Science Review*, 91/1 (March 1997), pp. 1–14

Maley, Michael, 'Absentee Voting', in Richard Rose (ed.), *International Encyclopedia of Elections* (Washington, DC: CQ Press, 2000)

Massicotte, Louis, 'Day of Election', in Richard Rose (ed.), *International Encyclopedia of Elections* (Washington, DC: CQ Press, 2000)

MORI, 'New Ways to Vote', 1 August 2003, <http://www.mori.com/polls/2003/electoralcommission.shtml>

Norris, Pippa, 'The Bridging and Bonding Role of Online Communities', *Harvard International Journal of Press Politics*, 7/3 (2002), pp. 3–8 (2002 a)

—*Democratic Phoenix: Political Activism Worldwide* (New York: Cambridge University Press, 2002) (2002 b)

—*Digital Divide: Civic Engagement, Information Poverty and the Internet Worldwide* (New York: Cambridge University Press, 2001)

—*Electoral Engineering: Electoral Rules and Voting Choices* (New

York: Cambridge University Press, forthcoming spring 2004)

— 'Preaching to the Converted? Pluralism, Participation and Party Websites', *Party Politics,* 9/1 (2003), pp. 21–45 (2003)

— 'Who Surfs? New Technology, Old Voters and Virtual Democracy in US Elections 1992–2000', in Elaine Kamarck and Joseph S. Nye (Jr), *Governance.com? Democracy in the Information Age,* revised edn (Washington, DC: Brookings Institution Press, 2002) (2002 c)

— and Sanders, David, 'Medium or Message? Campaign Learning during the 2001 British General Election', *Political Communications* (forthcoming 2004)

Powell, G. Bingham (Jr), 'American Voter Turnout in Comparative Perspective', *American Political Science Review,* 80/1 (1986), pp. 17–43

Rash, Wayne (Jr), *Politics on the Net: Wiring the Political Process* (New York: W. H. Freeman, 1997)

Rheingold, Howard, *The Virtual Community: Homesteading on the Electronic Frontier* (Reading, Mass.: Addison Wesley, 1993)

Schwartz, Edward, *Netactivism: How Citizens Use the Internet* (Sebastapol, Calif.: Songline Studios, 1996)

Solop, F. I., 'Digital Democracy Comes of Age: Internet Voting and the 2000 Arizona Democratic Primary Election', *PS-Political Science and Politics,* 34/2 (2001), pp. 289–93

Stratford, J. S. and Stratford, J., 'Computerized and Networked Government Information', *Journal of Government Information,* 28/3 (2001), pp. 297–301

UK Electoral Commission, *The Shape of Elections to Come* (London: Electoral Commission, 31 July 2003), <http://www.electoralcommission.gov.uk>

— *Modernising Elections: A Strategic Evaluation of the 2002 Electoral Pilot Schemes* (London, 2002), <http://www.electoralcommission.gov.uk>

Part II: Country by Country

Voter Turnout Country by Country

This section should be read in conjunction with the tables in Part III, which summarize voter turnout in all types of elections country by country, and the ranking tables which follow them.

Part II: Country By Country

Austria

Electoral system for the national Parliament (lower house)	List proportional representation
The national legislature is	Bicameral
Number of seats in the national Parliament	183
Number of women in the national Parliament	62 of 183 (33.9%) as of January 2004
Presidential elections	Yes
Accession to the European Union	1995

AUSTRIA HAS HAD A VERY HIGH voter turnout in the period since the Second World War. The average turnout for parliamentary elections since 1945 is almost 91 per cent, which is higher than those of most other countries in Europe, or elsewhere in the world. On a global ranking list of voter turnout Austria ranks tenth, and on a regional ranking list of voter turnout in Western Europe it ranks second. Most of the countries in the world that have higher levels of voter turnout than Austria have compulsory voting, which was formerly practised in Austria for national elections but was abolished in most regions of the country in 1979. Only two, Vorarlberg and Tirol, retained compulsory voting until 2004. These two regions have usually shown a higher voter turnout than the rest of the country in recent years.

Looking at the turnout trend in Austria since 1945, there are some exceptions to the trend of high turnout. The most recent parliamentary elections show some decline in turnout, which started in the 1980s. Over the 1990s, the average declined by approximately 7 per cent.

A similar trend can be found for presidential elections, where turnout has also declined, by 15 per cent since 1980 and by several percentage points even before then.

Parliamentary elections were due to be held in late 2003, but were called when the governing coalition between the Freedom Party and the Austrian People's Party broke up in September 2002. The elections that followed gave the People's Party 43 per cent of the seats in Parliament—its biggest electoral success in two decades.

Austria has taken part in two elections to the European Parliament, in 1996 and 1999, and these have seen a significantly lower turnout than the national parliamentary or presidential elections. Austria is around the middle on a ranking table of member countries' turnout in European Parliament elections. The Austrian average turnout in both kinds of election is almost 59 per cent—just below the European average of 60.6 per cent.

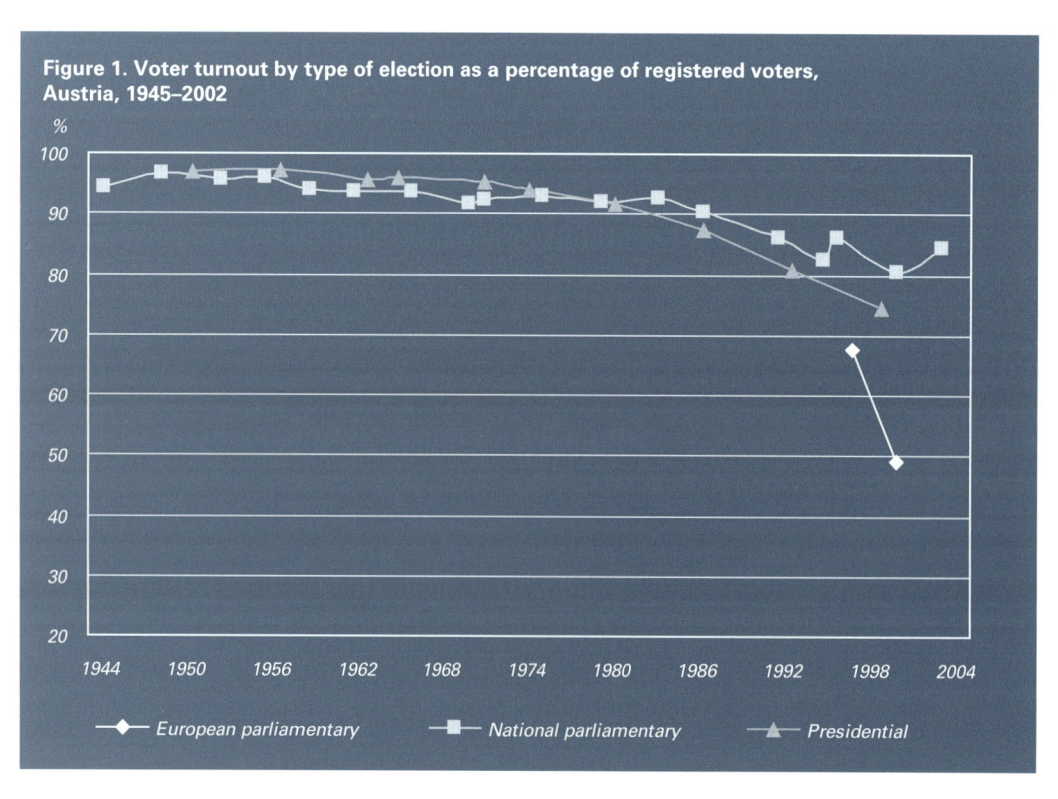

Figure 1. Voter turnout by type of election as a percentage of registered voters, Austria, 1945–2002

Voter Turnout in Western Europe

Belgium

Electoral system for the national Parliament (lower house)	List proportional representation
The national legislature is	Bicameral
Number of seats in the national Parliament	150
Number of women in the national Parliament	53 of 150 (35.3%) as of January 2004
Presidential elections	No
Accession to the European Union	Founder

AVERAGE VOTER TURNOUT IN national elections in Belgium has been the highest in Western Europe since 1945: it has never been below 90 per cent. Only Liechtenstein (which is not covered in the statistical summaries in this report) has a higher average turnout in national elections. Belgium also ranks fifth on a global ranking list of average turnout. The main reason for the high turnout would appear to be the practice of compulsory voting. Belgium was one of the first countries in the world to introduce compulsory voting, doing so as early as 1893, and any unjustified abstention is punishable by fines or by removal from the electoral register. This high turnout is, however, accompanied by a relatively high proportion of invalid and blank votes, among the largest in Western Europe. Nineteen parliamentary elections have been held in Belgium since 1945.

The 1999 parliamentary election in Belgium took place at the same time as the election to the European Parliament. One of the main issues during the campaign focused on the dioxin-in-food crisis resulting from polluted animal feed. The outgoing government had had a certain success, for example, in reducing unemployment and the public debt, and the country joined the European single currency in 2002. After the 1999 election the Liberal Party became the leading force in the House of Representatives for the first time since the Second World War, but formed a coalition government with five other parties. The electoral campaign leading up to the most recent election, in 2003, was mainly focused on tax issues and tax cuts. During its four years in government the coalition had also introduced some very progressive legislation. The Liberal Party and the Socialist Party renewed their agreement and formed a new coalition.

Belgium is a founding member of the European Union. It has experienced five elections to the European Parliament and turnout for these elections is the highest among all the member states—above 91 per cent, which is only one one percentage point lower than the average turnout in national elections in Belgium (a little over 92 per cent).

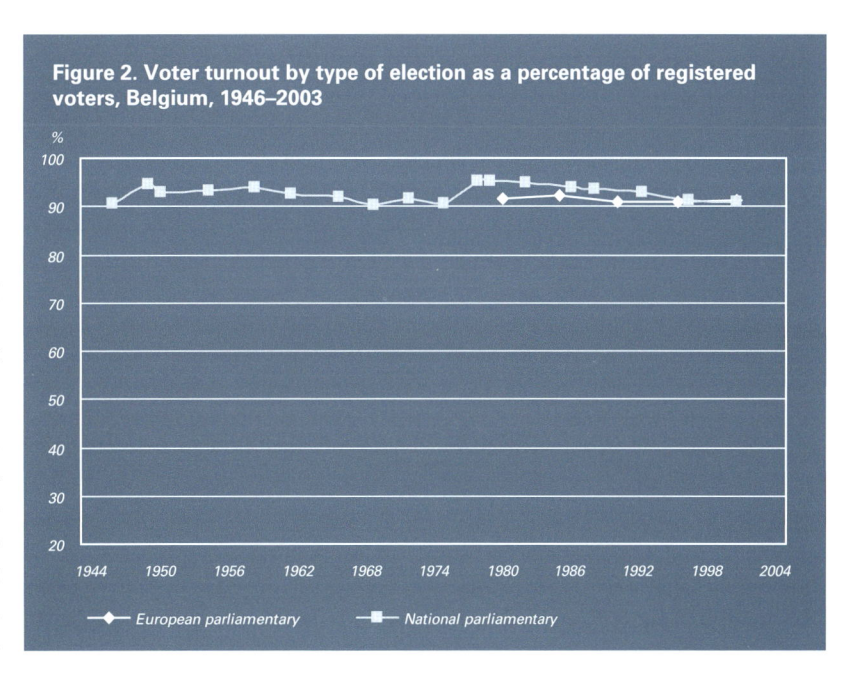

Figure 2. Voter turnout by type of election as a percentage of registered voters, Belgium, 1946–2003

Part II: Country By Country

Denmark

Electoral system for the national Parliament	List proportional representation
The national legislature is	Unicameral
Number of seats in the national Parliament	179
Number of women in the national Parliament	68 of 179 (38.0%) as of January 2004
Presidential elections	No
Accession to the European Union	1973

DENMARK HAS HAD STABLE VOTER TURNOUT during the post-Second World War period. Average turnout for parliamentary elections has been approximately 86 per cent with a variation of not more than 7 per cent throughout the years. This consistently high average turnout is an achievement for a country which does not practise compulsory voting, especially since Denmark has held more parliamentary elections since 1945 than any other EU member state (23 elections). The highest turnout ever measured in Denmark was in 1968 when 89 per cent of the voters turned out to vote.

On a global ranking list of average voter turnout Denmark ranks 32, but on a similar list for Western Europe it ranks eighth. Only very few of the countries that rank higher than Denmark in Western Europe do not practise compulsory voting.

The most recent parliamentary election was that of 2001. Turnout was relatively high at over 87 per cent. This was the first time county and municipal elections were held at the same time as the parliamentary elections. The nine-year-long rule of the Social Democrats ended with this election. Issues regarding immigration and the issue of family reunification as a basis for permitting immigration to Denmark dominated the campaign. A minority right-wing coalition government was formed after the election. As a monarchy, Denmark does not have presidential elections.

Women voters in Denmark turn out to vote to the same extent as men, but young Danish voters tend to start voting earlier than they did in the 1940s and 1950s. Turnout at municipal elections, however, is much lower than in national elections. The difference is approximately 15 per cent, and the groups that turn out to vote to a lesser extent at municipal elections include the unmarried, those on low incomes and those who have taken early retirement.

The proportion of invalid and blank votes cast is very low in Denmark—usually well below 1 per cent. Postal voting is allowed, but is not used to the same extent as in other Nordic countries.

Denmark joined the EU in 1973 and has so far experienced five elections to the European Parliament-the same number as the founding member states. As in most other member states, turnout in these elections has been much lower than that for elections to the national Parliament: the average for the five elections to the European Parliament is barely 50 per cent. This places Denmark tenth on a ranking list of average turnout at elections to the European Parliament.

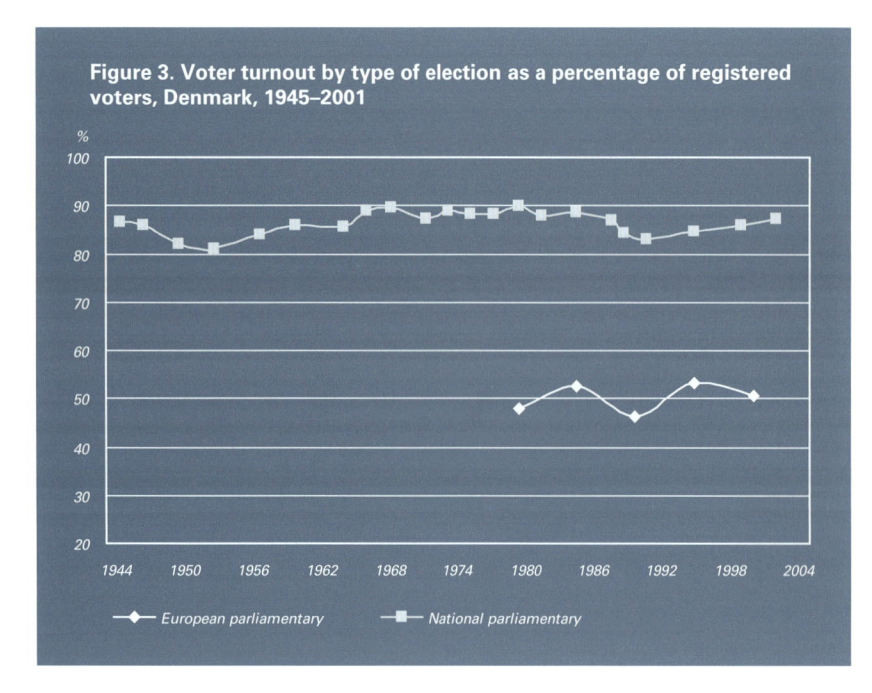

Figure 3. Voter turnout by type of election as a percentage of registered voters, Denmark, 1945–2001

Finland

Electoral system for the national Parliament	List proportional representation
The national legislature is	Unicameral
Number of seats in the national Parliament	200
Number of women in the national Parliament	75 of 200 (37.5%) as of January 2004
Presidential elections	Yes
Accession to the European Union	1995

TURNOUT IN THE FINNISH PARLIAMENTARY election of March 2003 was almost 70 per cent, which is a few percentage points higher than turnout at the three preceding elections held during the 1990s. Turnout declined somewhat during the 1990s, having been slightly higher in the 1960s and the early 1970s in particular. In the 17 parliamentary elections held since 1945, average turnout has been approximately 76 per cent. The highest turnout ever measured in Finland was 85.1 per cent at the parliamentary election in 1962. On a global ranking list Finland ranks 71. Average turnout at presidential elections is somewhat lower at around 74 per cent.

At the most recent election, in March 2003, the Center Party increased the number of its seats in Parliament by eight. The National Coalition Party lost a number of seats and other parties received approximately the same number of seats as at the last election.

The region of Åland—a number of islands which formally belong to Finland but as an autonomous region—has one reserved seat in the Parliament. The candidate for this seat is elected by the first-past-the-post system, although the electoral system used for national elections is a list proportional system.

Finland, like the other Nordic countries, has a very high proportion of women members of Parliament (MPs). Of all the countries in the world, only Denmark, Sweden and lately also Rwanda have a higher proportion of women MPs than Finland. The first woman president in Finland was elected in 2000 and as a result of the 2003 parliamentary election the country had its first woman prime minister as well, although she was obliged to step down shortly afterwards.

Another similarity with the other Nordic countries is the widespread practice of postal voting. All five Nordic countries have allowed postal voting (today abolished in Norway) for national elections, and in most cases for local and regional elections as well. At the most recent parliamentary election in Finland this option was used by almost 30 per cent of voters—quite a high percentage.

Elections to the European Parliament show quite an interesting pattern of turnout in Finland. The country has held elections to the European Parliament twice since joining the EU in 1995. At the first, in 1996, a turnout of almost 58 per cent was recorded. This fell dramatically in 1999, to only 30 per cent.

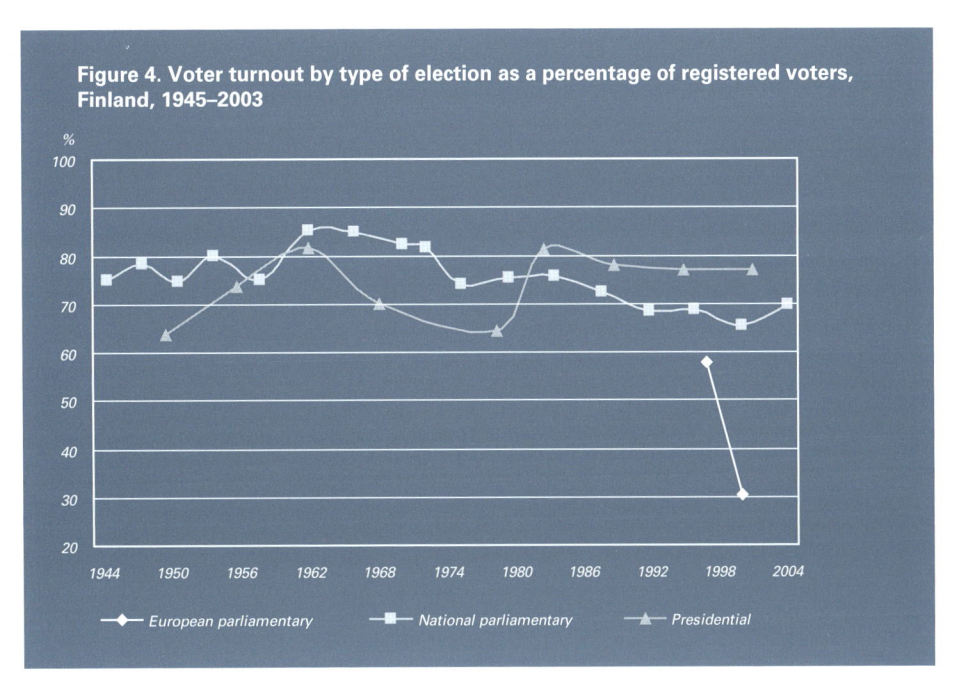

Figure 4. Voter turnout by type of election as a percentage of registered voters, Finland, 1945–2003

Part II: Country By Country

France

Electoral system for the national Parliament (lower house)	Two-round system
The national legislature is	Bicameral
Number of seats in the national Parliament	574
Number of women in the national Parliament	70 of 574 (12.2%) as of January 2004
Presidential elections	Yes
Accession to the European Union	Founder

THE MOST RECENT PARLIAMENTARY ELECTION in France took place in 2002. It was held shortly after the presidential election, where sixteen candidates competed in its first round and the leader of the National Front competed against the leader of the Rally for the Republic in the second round. Turnout at that parliamentary election was just above 60 per cent, which is relatively low for a West European country. Turnout for parliamentary elections in France has traditionally been higher—on average approximately 75 per cent since 1945. Only three other West European countries examined in this report show a lower average turnout than France. Turnout has declined throughout the years in France, but the average is still higher than that of many countries in, for example, Latin America and Africa.

France is one of the few West European countries that have presidential elections. These are held every five years. Interestingly, turnout is usually higher for presidential elections than for other types of election in France: the average is approximately 82 per cent. In the second round of the latest presidential election, in 2002, it was almost 80 per cent, because of intense voter interest in the contest between the incumbent president, Jacques Chirac, and the far right candidate Jean-Marie le Pen.

France is a founding member of the EU and has experienced five elections to the European Parliament. Here, as in almost all member countries, turnout is relatively low—on average around 53 per cent—and showing a declining trend at the most recent election.

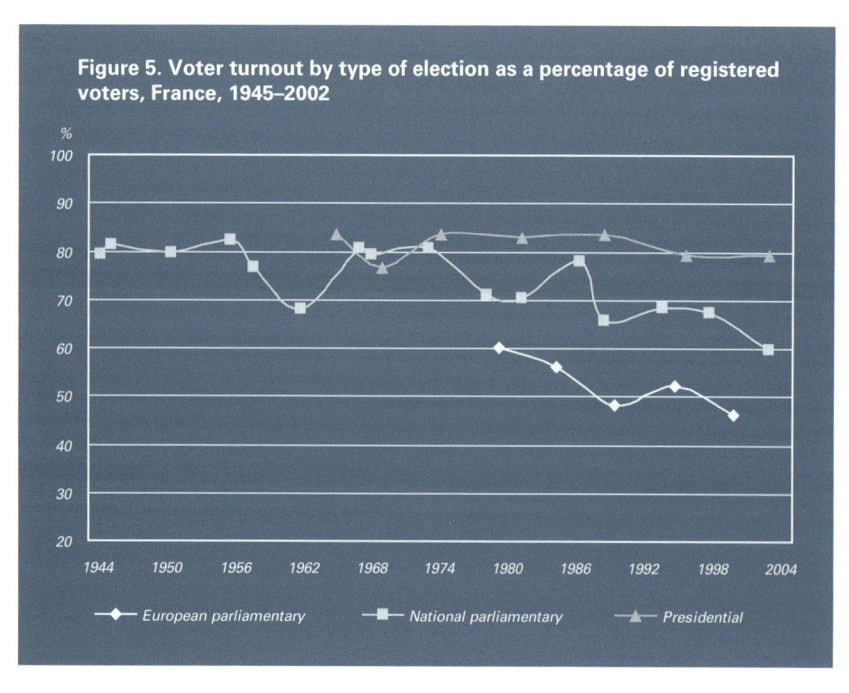

Figure 5. Voter turnout by type of election as a percentage of registered voters, France, 1945–2002

Voter Turnout in Western Europe

Germany

Electoral system for the national Parliament (lower house)	Mixed member proportional
The national legislature is	Bicameral
Number of seats in the national Parliament	at least 600. Currently 603
Number of women in the national Parliament	194 of 603 (32.2%) as of January 2004
Presidential elections	No
Accession to the European Union	Founder

IN GERMANY SINCE 1945 turnout for national parliamentary elections has varied between 77 per cent and 91 per cent. Fifteen national elections have been held during this time; the highest turnout was that of 1972, at 91.1 per cent. The most recent election in 2002 saw a turnout of 79 per cent. Germany's average turnout of 85 per cent places it tenth in Western Europe and just above the European average. Almost half of the European countries that have a higher average turnout have compulsory voting.

Germany has Western Europe's largest electorate—a little over 61 million voters. In 2002 German voters went to the polls after a debate which focused on the disastrous floods that had hit the country in the same year, and unemployment and the country's economy were also on the agenda. For the first time in German history, television showed a debate between the two main candidates for the post of chancellor. The Social Democratic Party and the Green Party formed a new coalition after the election.

As a founding member state of the EU, Germany has experienced five elections to the European Parliament. Average turnout is 58 per cent but turnout has declined at almost every election. It started at 65 per cent in 1979 but in 1999 turnout had declined by 20 percentage points compared with 1979, to 45 per cent.

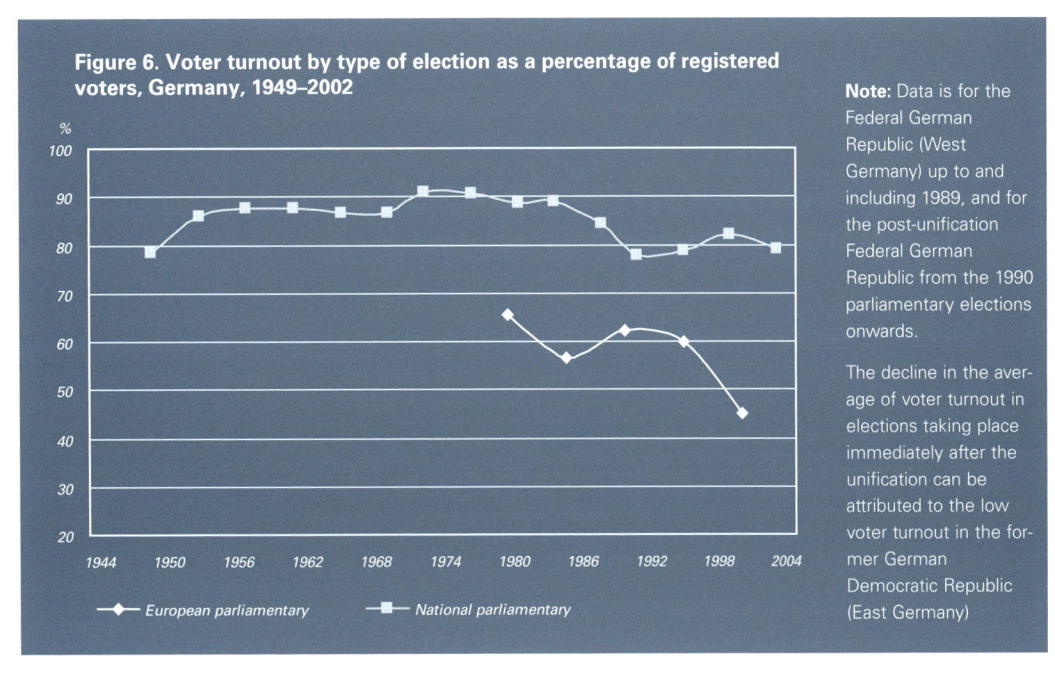

Figure 6. Voter turnout by type of election as a percentage of registered voters, Germany, 1949–2002

Note: Data is for the Federal German Republic (West Germany) up to and including 1989, and for the post-unification Federal German Republic from the 1990 parliamentary elections onwards.

The decline in the average of voter turnout in elections taking place immediately after the unification can be attributed to the low voter turnout in the former German Democratic Republic (East Germany)

Part II: Country By Country

Greece

Electoral system for the national Parliament	List proportional representation
The national legislature is	Unicameral
Number of seats in the national Parliament	300
Number of women in the national Parliament	26 of 300 (8.67%) as of January 2004
Presidential elections	No
Accession to the European Union	1981

GREECE SHOWS A FAIRLY HIGH TURNOUT at parliamentary elections. One reason for this may be the practice of compulsory voting. Sanctions are imposed on non-voters, although currently they are not strictly enforced in practice. The most recent national parliamentary election took place in 2000, and turnout—75 per cent—was the lowest since the 1950s. Turnout was very high in the 1980s but has declined by several percentage points since then. Average turnout in Greece since the first election in 1946 is 80 per cent, which is relatively high compared to the rest of the world. Sixteen elections have been held since 1946.

The outcome of the 2000 parliamentary election was a victory for the Panhellenic Socialist Movement (PASOK) which won almost 44 per cent of the seats. Four different parties are represented in Parliament, out of 26 that contested the election. In 2004, PASOK came out as the second largest party as it lost a few seats in Parliament and 4 per cent of the votes. New Democracy, the second largest party from 2000, won 45 per cent of the votes and the largest number of seats in Parliament.

Greece has the lowest proportion of women MPs among the countries included in this report. Between 8 and 9 per cent of the Greek MPs are women—26 out of a total of 300 MPs.

Greece joined the EU in 1981, and held its first elections to the European Parliament the same year, two years later than those in the other member states. Greece has thus experienced the same number of elections to the European Parliament as the founding members of the EU. It is one of the few member states that show a fairly stable trend in turnout for European Parliament elections—on average 78 per cent, which is among the highest averages among the member states. Greece ranks fourth on a ranking list of average turnout at elections to the European Parliament.

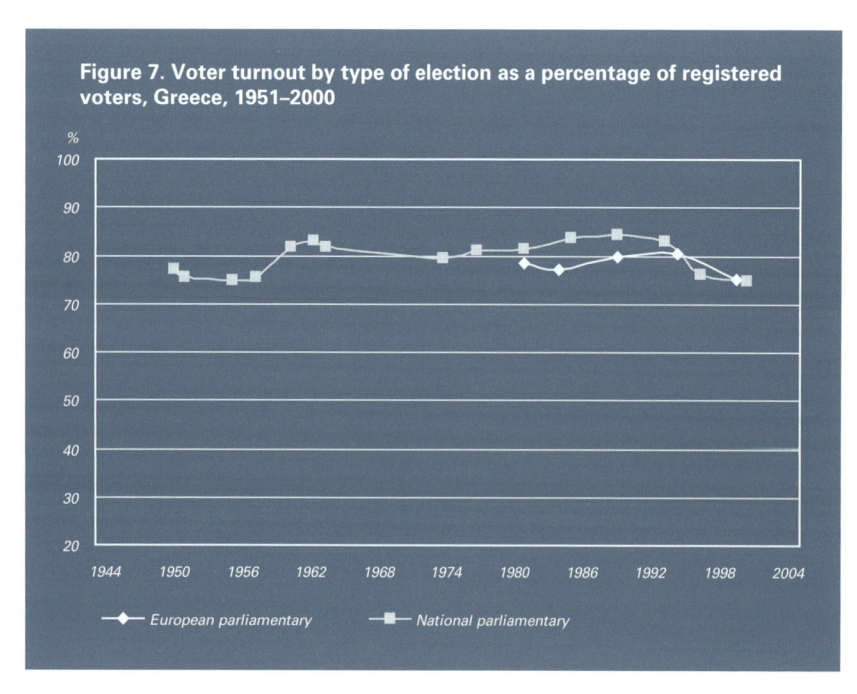

Figure 7. Voter turnout by type of election as a percentage of registered voters, Greece, 1951–2000

Iceland

Electoral system for the national Parliament	List proportional representation
The national legislature is	Unicameral
Number of seats in the national Parliament	63
Number of women in the national Parliament	19 of 63 (30.2%) as of January 2004
Presidential elections	Yes
Accession to the European Union	Not a member

THIS ISLAND NATION IS ONE out of four countries covered in this report that are not members of the EU. It is one of the smaller European countries in terms of both geographical size and population. Iceland became independent from Denmark in 1944 and, with an electorate of only 200,000 voters, has held 18 parliamentary elections since 1946.

Parliamentary elections take place every four years, as do presidential elections in principle. However, presidential elections have only taken place five times since 1952, usually because there have not been enough candidates standing. This was the case, for example, in 2000, the most recent occasion when the presidential term expired.

At the parliamentary election in 1999, some new groupings of parties emerged. The ruling centre–right coalition was challenged by the newly founded left bloc. The main issues during the campaign were related to domestic economic issues. In 2003 the campaign was focused on mainly EU membership and taxes. Iceland's economy had grown, and inflation and taxes were low compared to other European countries. The coalition formed in 1999 continued in government also after the 2004 elections. Turnout in 1999 was 84 per cent, the lowest ever recorded at a parliamentary election in Iceland, although this should not be considered low in comparative terms. In 2003, turnout increased to 87 per cent which is closer to average Icelandic standard. Historically, voter turnout in Iceland has been high. Although it has fallen a little in recent years, average turnout since 1946 is almost 90 per cent, and the highest voter turnout ever recorded in a Nordic country was that at the parliamentary election in Iceland in 1956. At 92.1 per cent, this must be considered very high in a country where compulsory voting has never been practised, and it places Iceland fifth on a European ranking list of average turnout. It should be noted that all countries that show higher average turnout have or have had some element of compulsory voting.

Most of the electoral management bodies in Western Europe are located in a government department. In Iceland the elections are run by the Ministry of Justice and Ecclesiastical Affairs which, apart from elections, handles judicial issues and issues concerning religion. The electoral administration works very well and runs elections at low cost. Iceland was one of the first countries in the world to introduce voting by mail. Voting by mail, or 'voting by letter', as it was first called, was introduced as early as 1914 for fishermen, sailors and similar groups who were temporarily away from their electoral district. The right to vote by mail was extended to the disabled, the elderly and others in 1923, and today it is possible for all voters to opt to vote in this way. Voting by mail has become a popular alternative among Icelandic voters and is used by approximately 20 per cent of voters.

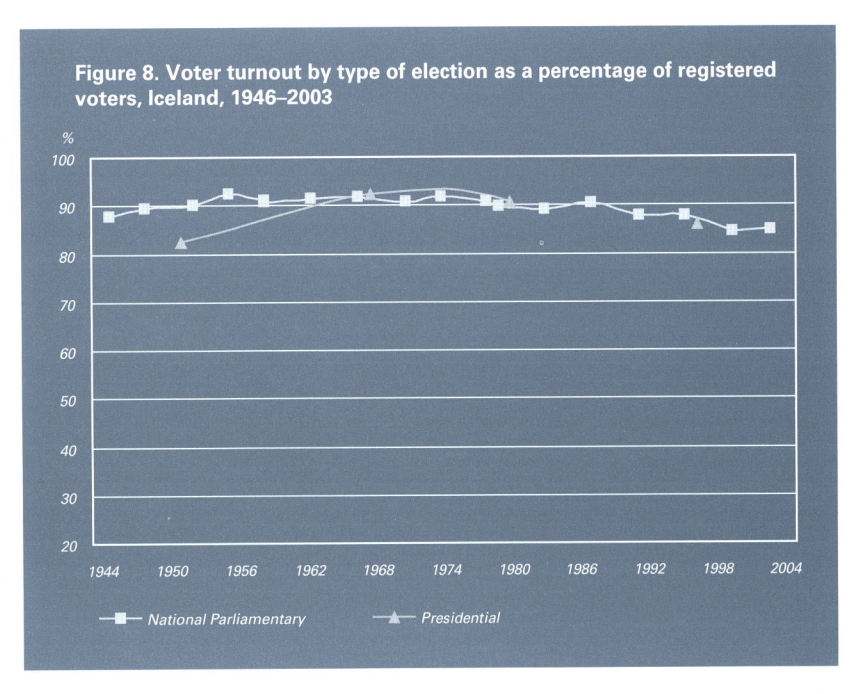

Figure 8. Voter turnout by type of election as a percentage of registered voters, Iceland, 1946–2003

Part II: Country By Country

Ireland

Electoral system for the national Parliament (lower house)	Single transferable vote
The national legislature is	Bicameral
Number of seats in the national Parliament	166
Number of women in the national Parliament	22 of 166 (13.3%) as of January 2004
Presidential elections	Yes
Accession to the European Union	1973

THE MOST RECENT PARLIAMENTARY ELECTION in Ireland is that of 2002. Voter turnout then was 62 per cent. Although Ireland has showed great variation in turnout as between different kinds of election, this was the lowest ever recorded at a parliamentary election in Ireland. On a European ranking list of average turnout only Switzerland shows a lower average turnout than Ireland. Ireland does far better on a global ranking list where it ranks around the middle.

On the other hand, the turnout trend at national parliamentary elections is fairly stable. It was above 70 per cent at all elections from 1948 up to and including the 1987 election, and since the 1989 election it has been below 70 per cent. However, the differences are not extreme and the average turnout over the past half-decade is 72.6 per cent.

Ireland has had six presidential elections since 1945. Turnout is usually much lower for presidential elections than it is for parliamentary elections: the average is around 57 per cent, which is roughly 15 per cent less than that for parliamentary elections and the lowest average for presidential elections in Western Europe. This may be because the president enjoys less power in Ireland than in most European countries.

Ireland is the only EU member state to use the single transferable vote (STV) system for both national elections and elections to the European Parliament. Compared to the other European countries covered in this report, it also has very low numbers of invalid or blank votes—usually well below 1 per cent.

Interestingly, at some elections to the European Parliament Ireland has shown a higher turnout than many other member states. However, its turnout at elections to the European Parliament has been the most unpredictable of all the member countries. For some elections it has been well below the European average.

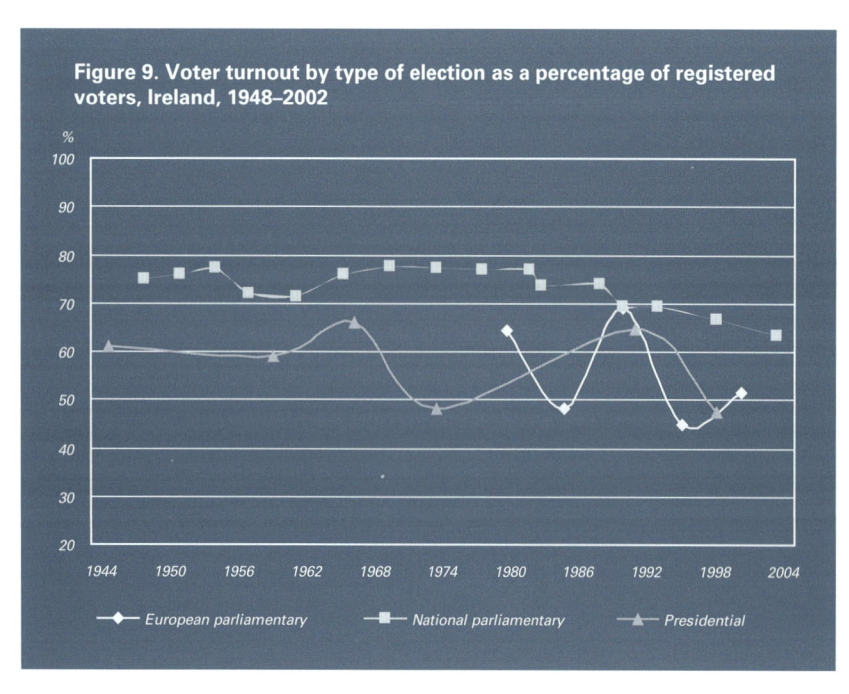

Figure 9. Voter turnout by type of election as a percentage of registered voters, Ireland, 1948–2002

Voter Turnout in Western Europe

Italy

Electoral system for the national Parliament (lower house)	Mixed member proportional
The national legislature is	Bicameral
Number of seats in the national Parliament	630
Number of women in the national Parliament	71 of 630 (11.5%) as of January 2004
Presidential elections	No
Accession to the European Union	Founder

ITALY SHOWS A FAIRLY STABLE TREND in voter turnout since 1946. The average turnout at parliamentary elections is almost 90 per cent. This is one of the highest in Western Europe and in the world. A slight decline in turnout has been seen recently, at parliamentary elections and at elections to the European Parliament.

The most recent parliamentary election in Italy took place in 2001. The outgoing Parliament was only the fifth to complete its five-year term since the Second World War. Fifteen parliamentary elections have been held in Italy since 1945. In the 2001 election the parties of the far right under the leadership of Silvio Berlusconi won an absolute majority of seats in the Chamber of Deputies and a simple majority in the Senate as a newly formed group under the name the House of Freedoms. After the EU imposed sanctions on Austria after the election there in 2000, when the country included a party of the far right in the government, concern increased within the EU about Italy as well.

The proportion of women MPs in the new Parliament in Italy is quite low compared to other European countries.

In recent years Italy has greatly reduced the number of polling stations as a result of changes in the electoral system and the system of electoral administration during the 1990s. This has resulted in crowds of voters queuing up to vote, not all of whom have been given the chance to cast their ballot, although voting hours have been extended. This was noted mainly at the 2000 regional elections.

Compulsory voting was practised in Italy previously but today voting is only considered a duty and no sanctions are imposed on non-voters.

Elections to the European Parliament also show a high turnout in Italy—on average almost 80 per cent, which places Italy third on a ranking list of EU member states.

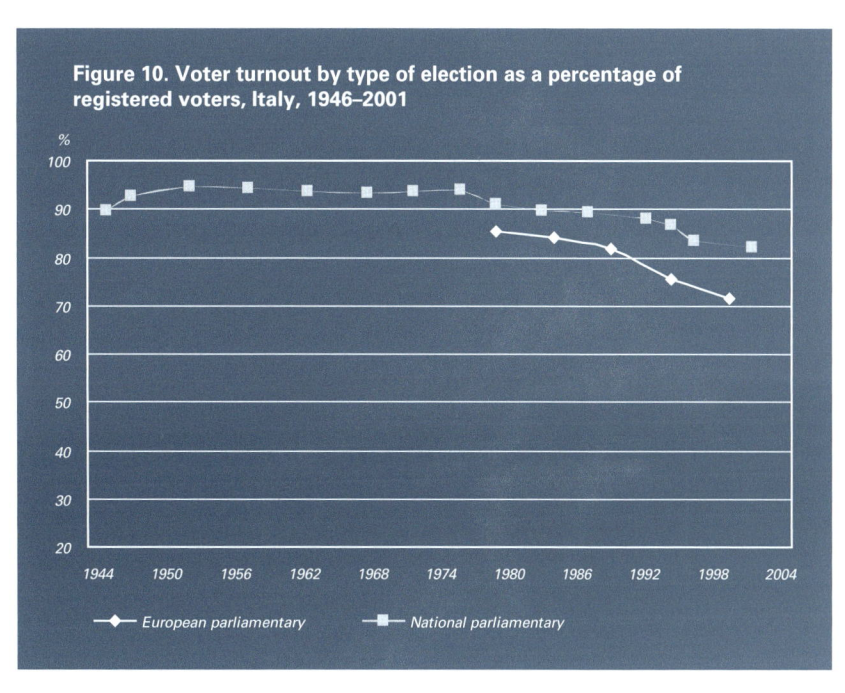

Figure 10. Voter turnout by type of election as a percentage of registered voters, Italy, 1946–2001

Part II: Country By Country

Luxembourg

Electoral system for the national Parliament	List proportional representation
The national legislature is	Unicameral
Number of seats in the national Parliament	60
Number of women in the national Parliament	10 of 60 (16.7%) as of January 2004
Presidential elections	No
Accession to the European Union	Founder

OF THE COUNTRIES EXAMINED in this report, Luxembourg has the smallest parliament and the second-smallest electorate. The Parliament consists of 60 seats, of which 10 are held by women. The electorate is just above 200,000, which is approximately the same size as those of Iceland and Malta.

Turnout in Luxembourg has remained very stable and high during the past decade in both parliamentary elections and elections to the European Parliament. Average turnout in parliamentary elections is almost 90 per cent. It has declined during recent years but only very little.

The most recent parliamentary election in Luxembourg took place in 1999. It led to some minor changes in government. The Christian Social Party held on to power as the largest party in Parliament, but the liberal Democratic Party overtook the Socialist Workers' Party as the second-largest party. Except for the two largest parties, which formed a new coalition government, four others are currently represented in the Parliament.

Luxembourg has had compulsory voting since 1919.

After Belgium, Luxembourg has the highest average turnout at elections to the European Parliament—almost 88 per cent on average since 1979 and never less than 85 per cent. All five elections to the European Parliament in which Luxembourg, a founding member state of the EU, has taken part have taken place on the same day as elections to the national Parliament.

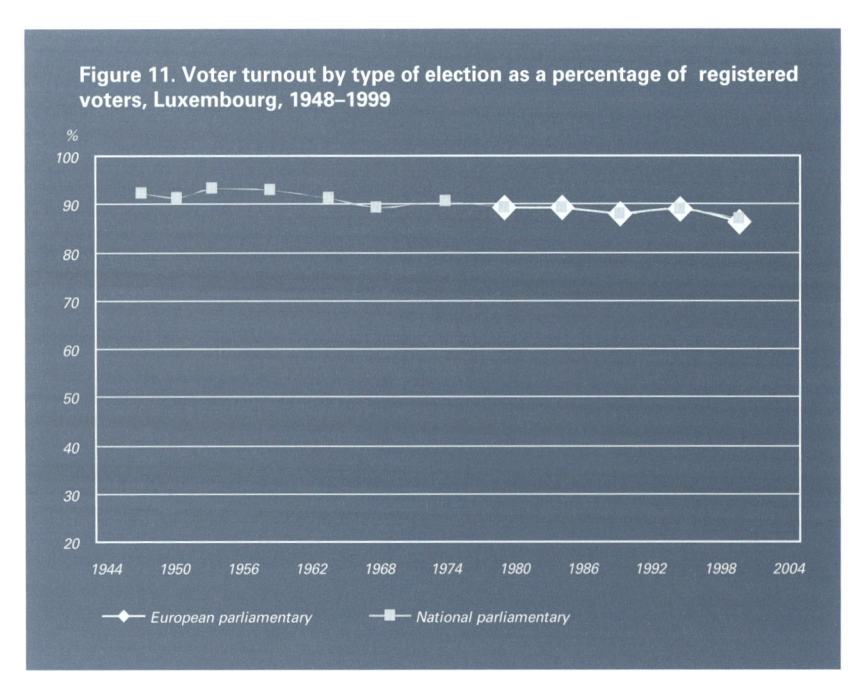

Figure 11. Voter turnout by type of election as a percentage of registered voters, Luxembourg, 1948–1999

Malta

Electoral system for the national Parliament	Single transferable vote
The national legislature is	Unicameral
Number of seats in the national Parliament	65
Number of women in the national Parliament	6 of 65 (9.2%) as of January 2004
Presidential elections	No
Accession to the European Union	Not a member

MALTA HAS BEEN CITED MANY TIMES by academics as an example of a country that has a very high voter turnout without having compulsory voting. Among the countries included in this report, of those that do not have compulsory voting, only Iceland shows a higher average turnout than Malta.

Fifteen parliamentary elections have been held since 1947. Turnout was much lower in the 1940s and 1950s than it is today: the first few elections after the Second World War showed turnouts of around 75 per cent, which is not regarded as low but is almost 20 per cent lower than turnout at the most recent election in 1998.

The highest turnout ever measured was in 1996, when more than 97 per cent of registered voters turned out to vote in the parliamentary election. Except for the first few elections after the Second World War, turnout in Malta has remained very stable over the years.

The 1998 election followed the premature dissolution of the Parliament less than two years after the previous election. There was only a one-month campaign and it focused mainly on possible membership of the EU and economic issues. Malta joined the EU on 1 May 2004.

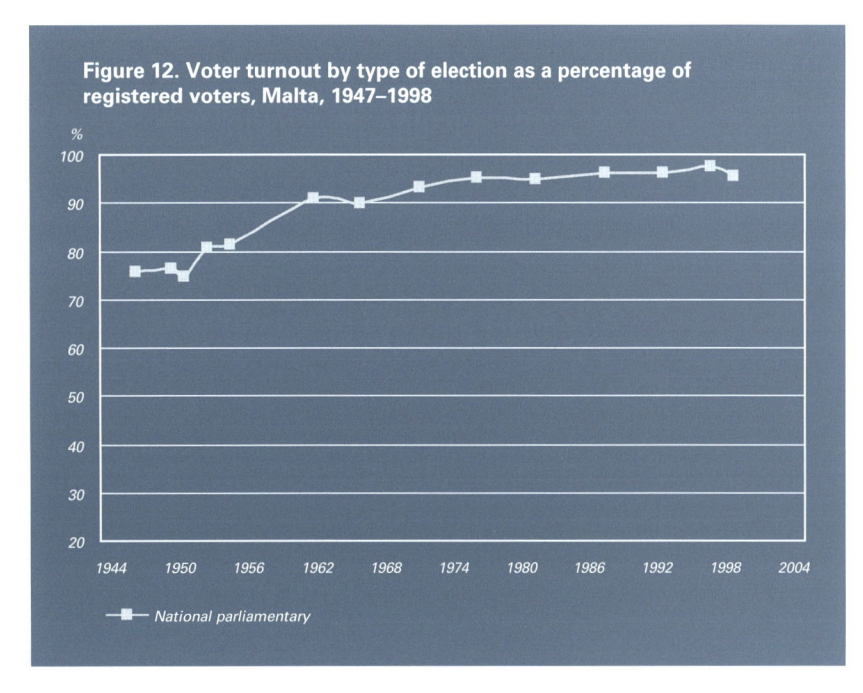

Figure 12. Voter turnout by type of election as a percentage of registered voters, Malta, 1947–1998

Part II: Country By Country

Netherlands

Electoral system for the national Parliament (lower house)	List proportional representation
The national legislature is	Bicameral
Number of seats in the national Parliament	150
Number of women in the national Parliament	55 of 150 (36.7%) as of January 2004
Presidential elections	No
Accession to the European Union	Founder

IT WAS COMPULSORY FOR CITIZENS to vote in national parliamentary elections until 1967 in the Netherlands, and this has left clear traces in the history of the country's voter turnout. Before 1970 the average turnout was 95 per cent, but after voting was made voluntary, starting with the next election in 1971, a clear decline in turnout is apparent. The average fell to 82 per cent. Still, the overall average turnout in the Netherlands since 1946 is almost 87 per cent, which places it fairly high up on a global ranking list of voter turnout and seventh on a ranking list of West European countries.

The Netherlands is one of the countries that have introduced new technology in their electoral processes and one of the first to introduce it on a national basis. It is possible today to vote using voting machines at the polling stations in most regions of the country.

The most recent parliamentary election in the Netherlands (in 2003) and the one before (in 2002) attracted international attention since the leader of one anti-immigration political party was shot dead a few days before the 2002 election. The 2003 election was called because of the premature dissolution of Parliament. This time the Labour Party increased the number of its seats in the Parliament, one less party is represented, and the party whose leader was assassinated, the List Pim Fortuyn, also lost a large share of its voters compared with the 2002 election.

A large proportion of Dutch MPs are women—almost 37 per cent, which is the fifth-largest share in the world. Only the Scandinavian countries Sweden, Denmark and Finland have a higher proportion of women MPs (as well as the African country Rwanda, after the recent introduction of quotas).

At elections to the European Parliament the Netherlands also shows a declining trend, but it has never been compulsory to vote at these elections. Turnout has fallen at each election to the European Parliament since the first took place in 1979. At 58 per cent in 1979 and 30 per cent in 1999, it has fallen by 5–10 per cent at each election.

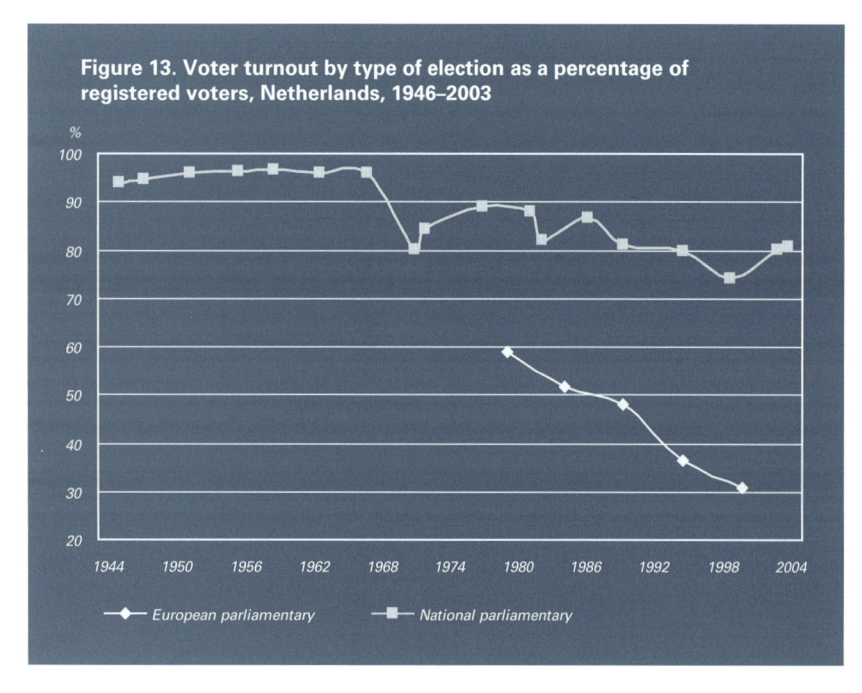

Figure 13. Voter turnout by type of election as a percentage of registered voters, Netherlands, 1946–2003

Voter Turnout in Western Europe

Norway

Electoral system for national Parliament	List proportional representation
The national legislature is	Unicameral
Number of seats in the national Parliament	165
Number of women in the national Parliament	60 of 165 (36.4%) as of January 2004
Presidential elections	No
Accession to the European Union	Not a member

AT THE MOST RECENT parliamentary election in Norway, in 2001, turnout was 75 per cent. This was the lowest ever recorded in a Norwegian parliamentary election since 1927 and it follows a trend of declining turnout in Norway since the beginning of the 1990s. Elections are held every four years and since 1945 there have been 15 elections. Average turnout, at around 80 per cent for parliamentary elections since 1945, is relatively high, at least compared to the rest of the world, although it is somewhat lower than the average in the other Nordic countries. On a ranking list of average turnout in Western Europe, Norway is just below the European average.

The campaign for the 2001 parliamentary election focused on two main issues, taxes and the state of the public services. Norwegian citizens pay some of the highest taxes in the world and, despite the fact that the UN has proclaimed Norway to have the highest standard of living in the world, the opposition parties argued that the income from oil exports should be used, among other things, to reduce taxes. The results of the election produced no absolute majority in the Parliament. A coalition was formed between the Conservatives, the Christian People's Party and the Liberal Left. The prime minister tendered his resignation. In the new Norwegian Parliament, which had its first sitting in October 2001, over 36 per cent of the MPs were women—comparatively a very high proportion.

Norway, like Ireland, has one of the lowest shares of invalid and blank votes in Europe: these usually account for well below 1 per cent of votes cast. At the last election 20 per cent of Norwegian voters voted before election day by mail or by other means. Postal voting was introduced only in 1997, although it was widely discussed during the 1970s and 1980s. However, postal voting had a short life in Norway. Following the restructuring of the public mail company and the new electoral law that was passed in 2002, it is no longer practised.

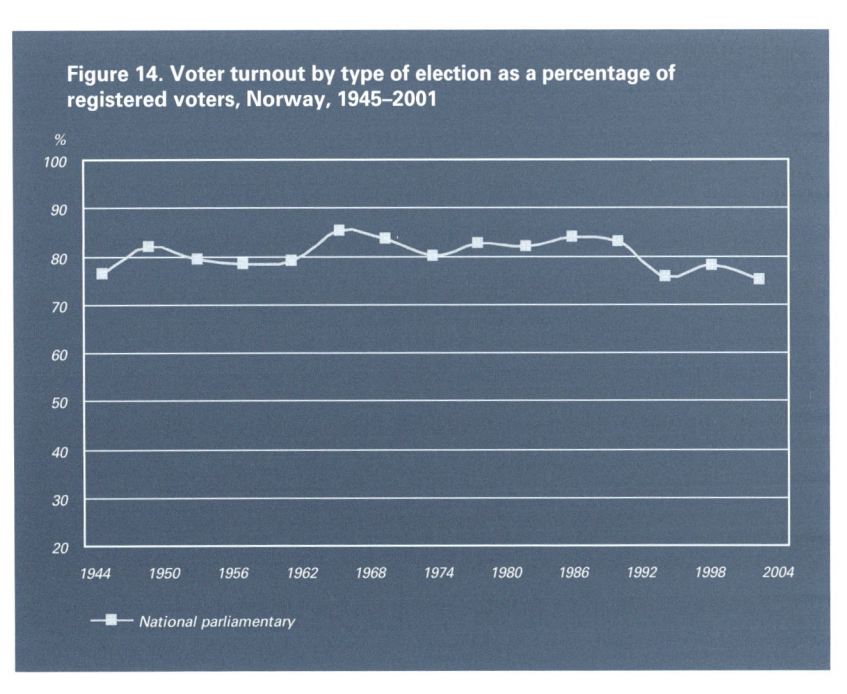

Figure 14. Voter turnout by type of election as a percentage of registered voters, Norway, 1945–2001

Part II: Country By Country

Portugal

Electoral system for the national Parliament	List proportional representation
The national legislature is	Unicameral
Number of seats in the national Parliament	230
Number of women in the national Parliament	44 of 230 (19.1%) as of January 2004
Presidential elections	Yes
Accession to the European Union	1986

PORTUGAL ACHIEVED A VERY HIGH voter turnout at its first election following the restoration of democracy in 1975. At 92 per cent it was among the highest levels in Europe since 1945. Since then, however, turnout has declined at almost every national election. The most obvious decline took place during the 1990s. At the most recent election, in 2002, turnout was 62 per cent. The average turnout at parliamentary elections since 1975 is almost 74 per cent.

Presidential elections in Portugal show lower turnouts than parliamentary elections. In the most recent presidential election in 2001 turnout was only 50 per cent. The average is approximately 69 per cent.

The most recent parliamentary election in 2002 was held following the premature dissolution of the Parliament in 2001. The prime minister had suddenly resigned in 2001 after his party was defeated in local elections the same year. During the campaign, perhaps not surprisingly, the focus was on economic issues: Portugal is still one of the poorest countries in the EU. The Social Democrats together with the People's Party formed a coalition as a result of the election.

Portugal has held four elections to the European Parliament since joining the EU in 1986. The average turnout at these elections is lower than that at national elections, at 50 per cent, but Portugal is one the few countries where turnout actually increased at the most recent election to the European Parliament, in 1999.

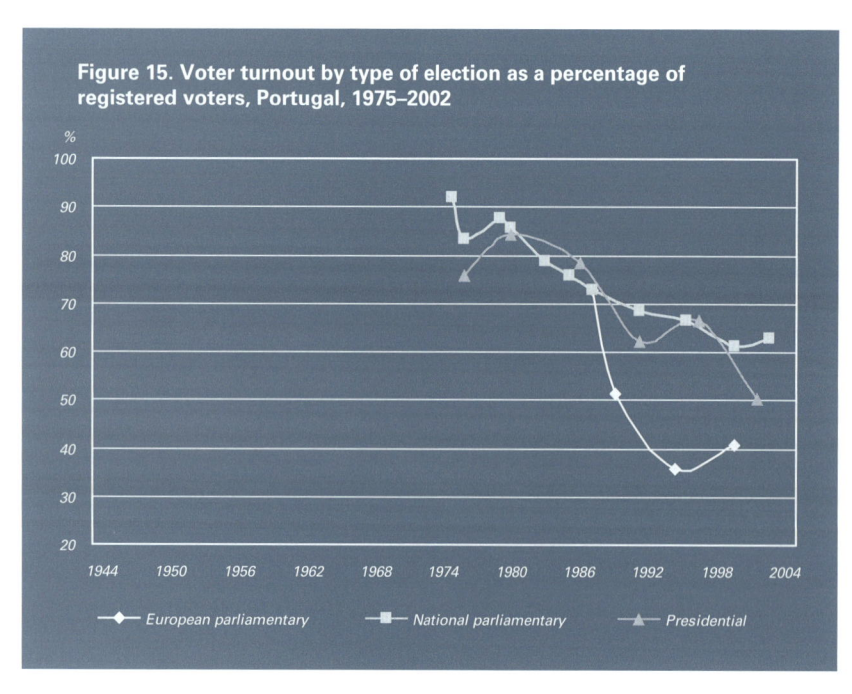

Figure 15. Voter turnout by type of election as a percentage of registered voters, Portugal, 1975–2002

Voter Turnout in Western Europe

Spain

Electoral system for the national Parliament (lower house)	List proportional representation
The national legislature is	Bicameral
Number of seats in the national Parliament	350
Number of women in the national Parliament	99 of 350 (28.3%) as of January 2004
Presidential elections	No
Accession to the European Union	1986

SPAIN HAS ONE OF THE LOWER LEVELS of turnout for parliamentary elections among the member states of the EU. The eight elections to the national Parliament held since 1977 have produced an average turnout of 75 per cent—still not very low compared to the rest of the world. As figure 16 shows, turnout at national elections declined at the most recent election, in 2000, to 68.7 per cent. Only once since 1977—at the second election held in Spain, in 1979—has turnout at a parliamentary election been so low.

The campaign leading up to the parliamentary election of 2000 was marked by bombings carried out by the Basque separatist movement Homeland and Liberty (Euzkadi Ta Azkatasuna, ETA). The car bombing during this campaign was the third since 1999.

The average turnout at the four elections to the European Parliament since 1986, when Spain joined the EU, is lower than that for national elections, at approximately 62 per cent, but still places Spain fifth on a ranking list of average turnout among the member states.

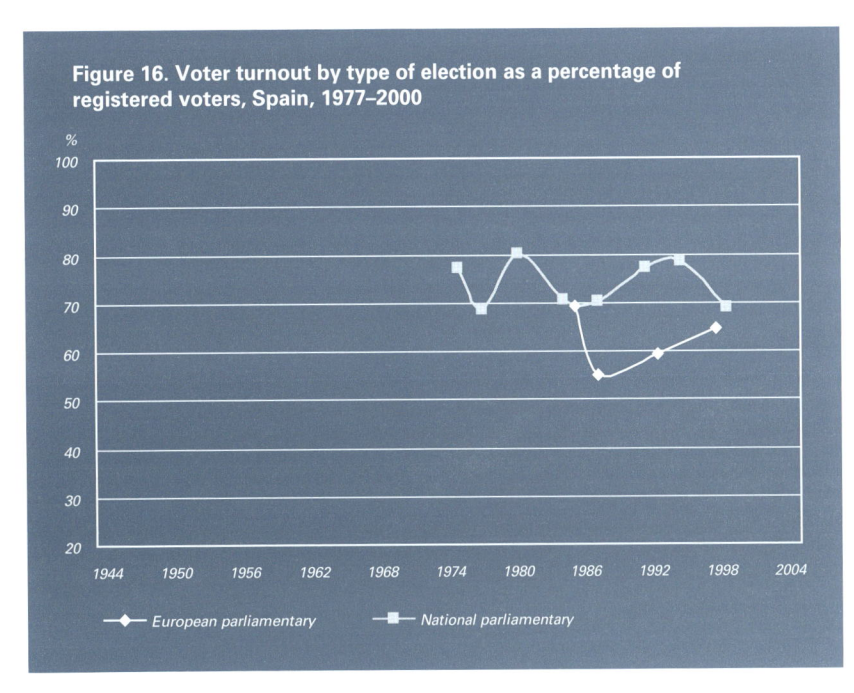

Figure 16. Voter turnout by type of election as a percentage of registered voters, Spain, 1977–2000

Part II: Country By Country

Sweden

Electoral system for the national Parliament	List proportional representation
The national legislature is	Unicameral
Number of seats in the national Parliament	349
Number of women in the national Parliament	158 of 349 (45.3%) as of January 2004
Presidential elections	No
Accession to the European Union	1995

VOTER TURNOUT HAS BEEN FAIRLY HIGH IN SWEDEN since 1945. Eighteen parliamentary elections have been held since then and the average turnout is almost 86 per cent. The pattern of high turnout held until the most recent parliamentary elections in 1998 and 2002, when turnout decreased to 81.4 and 80.1 per cent, respectively. The highest turnout ever in Sweden was in 1976, when a conservative government came to power for the first time in 40 years. At almost 92 per cent, this was the second-highest ever recorded in the Nordic countries, after the election in Iceland in 1963. For national elections Sweden ranks ninth on a European ranking list of average turnout. The declining turnout at parliamentary elections, as well as elections to the European Parliament, has generated much debate among politicians and academics and in the media about low participation and how to increase turnout.

The number of women represented in Parliament has been high over recent decades, and Sweden is at the top of a ranking list showing the proportion of women in parliament. The most recent election, in 2002, resulted in a slight increase in the proportion of women MPs, which is now 45 per cent. In 1999 Sweden was the first country in the world to have more women ministers than men.

The parliamentary election in 2002 resulted in a third term for the prime minister, who is also the leader of the Social Democratic Party. The party formed a minority government as agreement with the smaller parties on a coalition was not possible. The conservative opposition party faced its worst election since the 1970s, while the Liberals did better than before.

Postal voting has been practised in Sweden since 1942 and 30 per cent of the voters voted by mail at the post office in the most recent (2002) parliamentary election. In the referendum on adopting the euro in 2003, it was almost 32 per cent.

Since joining the EU, Sweden has held only two elections to the European Parliament. In contrast to the parliamentary elections, these elections show a very low turnout—on average 40 per cent, which is the second-lowest turnout in Europe (the United Kingdom having the lowest). The last election to the European Parliament in Sweden, in 1999, produced a turnout of only 38 per cent, which is one of the lowest ever for these elections.

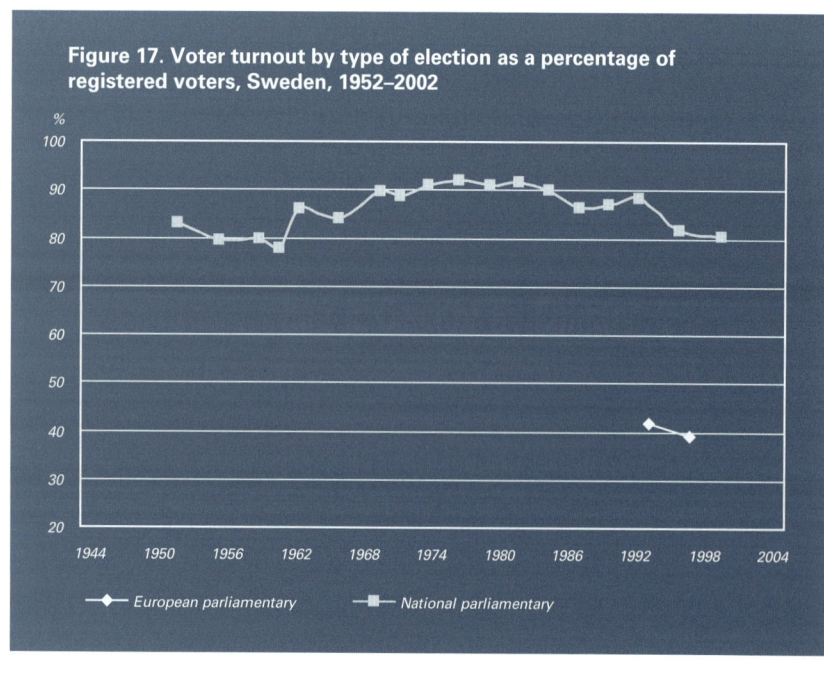

Figure 17. Voter turnout by type of election as a percentage of registered voters, Sweden, 1952–2002

Switzerland

Electoral system for the national Parliament (lower house)	List proportional representation
The national legislature is	Bicameral
Number of seats in the national parliament	200
Number of women in the national parliament	46 of 200 (23.0%) as of January 2004
Presidential elections	No
Accession to the European Union	Not a member

SWITZERLAND IS FAMOUS for its many referendums and for this form of direct democracy, but its voter turnout is the lowest in Western Europe and one of the lowest in the world. The average turnout at parliamentary elections in Switzerland has been almost 57 per cent since 1947. From a turnout of almost 72 per cent in 1947, the lowest ever—42 per cent—was recorded in 1995, and at the most recent parliamentary election, in 1999, it was approximately 45 per cent. The trend is clearly declining: every decade since the 1940s, turnout has fallen by a few percentage points.

Compulsory voting was formerly practised in Switzerland. Once it was abolished, a few cantons decided to continue this practice but today only the canton of Schaffhausen has compulsory voting (as it has had since 1904).

Postal voting is used extensively at most elections in Switzerland, and is a growing practice in towns and suburbs. On average in the country, a little more than 50 per cent of the voters choose to vote by mail. There are, however, differences between the cantons. In Geneva and Basle, for example, more than 95 per cent of voters voted by mail in the most recent election, while in places such as Valais or Ticino only a small percentage chose to do so. In several of regions where access to postal voting was simplified ten years ago, turnout has increased.

Switzerland has recently completed pilot projects trying out e-voting. This includes voting on the Internet, by using the telephone, by SMS/text messages and so on. This has mainly been tried at elections in Geneva, but other regions such as Zurich and Neuchatel have also started to test new technology in the electoral process.

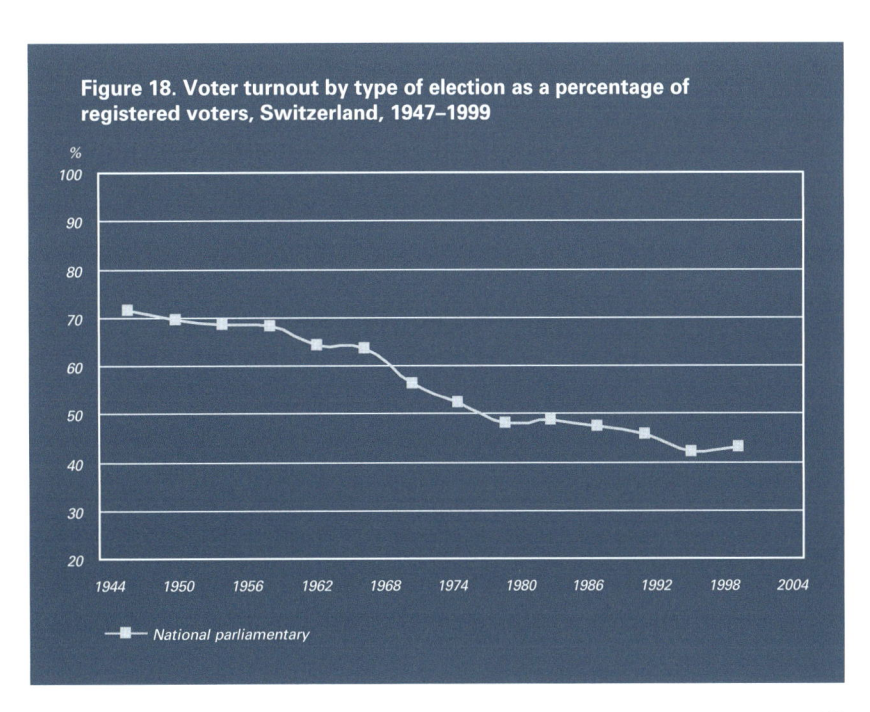

Figure 18. Voter turnout by type of election as a percentage of registered voters, Switzerland, 1947–1999

Part II: Country By Country

United Kingdom

Electoral system for the national Parliament (lower house)	First past the post
The national legislature is	Bicameral
Number of seats in the national parliament	659
Number of women in the national parliament	118 of 659 (17.9%) as of January 2004
Presidential elections	No
Accession to the European Union	1973

At the most recent election in the United Kingdom, in 2001, turnout declined by several percentage points, to 59 per cent—the lowest ever since the introduction of universal suffrage. It has declined at each of the two latest elections in the UK. The highest levels of turnout were measured in the 1950s.

The UK has a maximum parliamentary term of five years, not a fixed term. The most recent parliamentary election in 2001 was called before the end of the parliamentary term, as is common practice. In addition, local elections in England and Northern Ireland had been postponed the month before because of the outbreak of foot-and-mouth disease. This was the first time since the Second World War that the British Government had decided to postpone elections. One of the main issues in the election campaign was the euro and whether the UK should at some point introduce the single European currency. Foot-and-mouth disease was also a major subject, as well as more traditional issues such as the improvement of schools, hospitals and other public services. The Labour Party won an absolute majority in Parliament.

The UK has experimented with introducing new technologies in the voting process. During the local elections in May 2002 pilot projects were run to try out new, innovative techniques such as remote electronic voting from any computer, touch-screen kiosks, voting by phone or text message, and voting at different public institutions such as libraries. One of the purposes was to increase participation in elections.

The parliamentary elections of 2001 were not the only elections in the British to produce a declining turnout. Turnout is low also at elections to the European Parliament. Although it is not a founding member of the EU, the British voters have voted at all five elections to the European Parliament. At the most recent election, in 1999, turnout was down at the record level of 24 per cent—the lowest ever for elections to the European Parliament in any of the member states. The average turnout in elections to the European Parliament in the UK is 32 per cent, while the average for national parliamentary elections is 75 per cent.

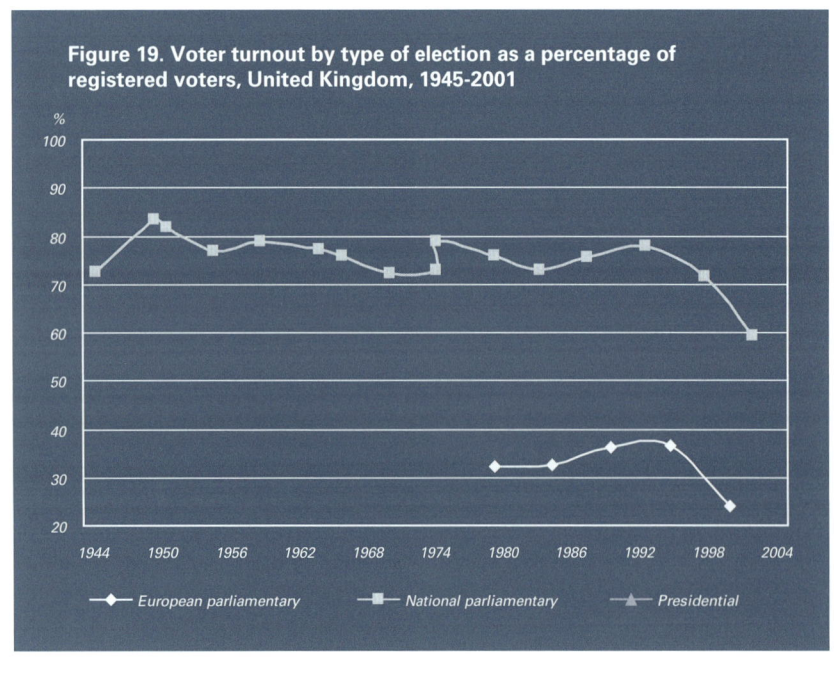

Figure 19. Voter turnout by type of election as a percentage of registered voters, United Kingdom, 1945-2001

Part III:
The International IDEA Database: Voter Turnout from 1945 to 2003

Part III: The International IDEA Database: Voter Turnout from 1945 to 2003

Definitions

Electoral System
The electoral system currently used by each country is shown in the table. This information is taken from the International IDEA Handbook of *Electoral System Design* (Stockholm: International IDEA, 1997).

Invalid
The number of invalid (and blank where applicable) votes, as reported by each country. More information on invalid and blank votes can be found at <http://www.aceproject.org>.

Population
The total population as described below under Voting Age Population.

Registration
The number of registered voters. The figure represents the number of names on the voters' register at the time the registration process closes, as reported by the electoral management body.

Total Vote
The total number of votes cast in the relevant election. More information on valid, invalid and blank votes can be found at the web site of the Administration and Cost of Elections (ACE) Project, http://www.aceproject.org.

Vote/Registration
The number of votes divided by the number of names on the voters' register, expressed as a percentage.

Vote/VAP
The number of votes divided by the Voting Age Population figure, expressed as a percentage.

Voter Turnout
Voter turnout is one measure of electoral participation. It is usually expressed as the percentage of eligible voters who cast a vote or 'turn out' at an election. The number of those who cast their vote includes those who cast blank or invalid votes, as they still participate.

The pool of eligible voters can be defined in different ways. International IDEA uses two measures: (a) the number of registered voters; and (b) the estimated voting age population (VAP). Information on the number of registered voters is compiled from information received from electoral management bodies around the world and estimates of voting age population are made using population statistics from the United Nations. There are advantages and disadvantages in both these calculations as the basis of turnout statistics. Registration is useful in that in many countries it is a prerequisite for voting, so that the number of registered voters reflects the number of those who may actually be able to cast a vote. However, in some countries there may be no system of registration or the register itself may be inaccurate.

The use of voting age population allows for an estimate of the potential number of voters if all systemic and administrative barriers were to be removed. However, as an estimate, it is not able to exclude those within a population who may not be eligible to register or to vote because of factors such as non-citizenship, mental competence or imprisonment.

For the purposes of this regional report all turnout statistics are presented as a percentage of registered voters.

Voting Age
The lowest age at which the right to vote is obtained in the country concerned.

Voting Age Population (VAP)
The estimated voting age population is based on the number of citizens in a country over the age of 18. It is not intended to be an exact measure of the VAP as it does not take into account legal or systemic barriers to the exercise of the franchise or account for non-eligible members of the population, such as resident non-citizens. It is intended as indicative only.

The VAPs shown here have been calculated from statistics produced by the Population Division of the UN Department of Economic and Social Affairs. Most estimates are based on the latest census data report in the UN *Demographic Yearbook 1998*.

PARLIAMENTARY ELECTIONS

1945–2003

Part III: The International IDEA Database: Voter Turnout from 1945 to 2003

Austria

YEAR	TOTAL VOTE	REGISTRATION	VOTE/REG
1945	3 253 329	3 449 605	94.3%
1949	4 250 616	4 391 815	96.8%
1953	4 395 519	4 586 870	95.8%
1956	4 427 711	4 614 464	96.0%
1959	4 424 658	4 696 603	94.2%
1962	4 506 007	4 805 351	93.8%
1966	4 583 970	4 886 818	93.8%
1970	4 630 851	5 045 841	91.8%
1971	4 607 616	4 984 448	92.4%
1975	4 662 684	5 019 277	92.9%
1979	4 784 173	5 186 735	92.2%
1983	4 922 454	5 316 436	92.6%
1986	4 940 298	5 461 414	90.5%
1991	4 848 741	5 628 912	86.1%
1994	4 760 987	5 774 000	82.5%
1995	4 959 539	5 768 009	86.0%
1999	4 695 192	5 838 373	80.4%
2002	4 982 261	5 912 592	84.3%

Belgium

YEAR	TOTAL VOTE	REGISTRATION	VOTE/REG
1946	2 460 796	2 724 796	90.3%
1949	5 320 263	5 635 452	94.4%
1950	5 219 276	5 635 452	92.6%
1954	5 463 130	5 863 092	93.2%
1958	5 575 127	5 954 858	93.6%
1961	5 573 861	6 036 165	92.3%
1965	5 578 876	6 091 534	91.6%
1968	5 554 652	6 170 167	90.0%
1971	5 741 270	6 271 240	91.5%
1974	5 711 996	6 322 227	90.3%
1977	6 005 195	6 316 292	95.1%
1978	6 039 916	6 366 652	94.9%
1981	6 504 056	6 878 141	94.6%
1985	6 552 234	7 001 297	93.6%
1987	6 573 045	7 039 250	93.4%
1991	6 623 897	7 144 884	92.7%
1995	6 562 149	7 199 440	91.1%

YEAR	TOTAL VOTE	REGISTRATION	VOTE/REG
1999	6 652 005	7 343 464	90.6%
2003	6 936 801	7 570 637	91.6%

Denmark

YEAR	TOTAL VOTE	REGISTRATION	VOTE/REG
1945	2 055 315	2 381 983	86.3%
1947	2 089 015	2 435 306	85.8%
1950	2 059 944	2 516 118	81.9%
1953	2 172 036	2 695 554	80.6%
1953	2 077 615	2 571 311	80.8%
1957	2 321 097	2 772 159	83.7%
1960	2 439 936	2 842 336	85.8%
1964	2 640 856	3 088 269	85.5%
1966	2 802 304	3 162 352	88.6%
1968	2 864 805	3 208 646	89.3%
1971	2 904 096	3 332 044	87.2%
1973	3 070 253	3 460 737	88.7%
1975	3 068 302	3 477 621	88.2%
1977	3 124 967	3 552 904	88.0%
1979	3 194 967	3 730 650	85.6%
1981	3 314 424	3 776 333	87.8%
1984	3 386 733	3 829 600	88.4%
1987	3 389 201	3 907 454	86.7%
1988	3 352 651	3 991 897	84.0%
1990	3 265 420	3 941 499	82.8%
1994	3 360 637	3 988 787	84.3%
1998	3 431 926	3 993 009	85.9%
2001	3 484 957	3 998 957	87.1%

Finland

YEAR	TOTAL VOTE	REGISTRATION	VOTE/REG
1945	1 710 251	2 284 249	74.9%
1948	1 893 837	2 420 287	78.2%
1951	1 825 779	2 448 239	74.6%
1954	2 019 042	2 526 969	79.9%
1958	1 954 397	2 606 258	75.0%
1962	2 310 090	2 714 838	85.1%

Voter Turnout in Western Europe

YEAR	TOTAL VOTE	REGISTRATION	VOTE/REG
1966	2 378 583	2 800 461	84.9%
1970	2 544 510	3 094 359	82.2%
1972	2 587 060	3 178 169	81.4%
1975	2 761 223	3 741 460	73.8%
1979	2 906 066	3 858 553	75.3%
1983	2 992 970	3 951 932	75.7%
1987	2 895 488	4 018 248	72.1%
1991	2 776 984	4 060 778	68.4%
1995	2 803 602	4 088 358	68.6%
1999	2 710 095	4 152 430	65.3%
2003	2 797 596	4 015 552	69.7%

France

YEAR	TOTAL VOTE	REGISTRATION	VOTE/REG
1945	19 657 603	24 622 862	79.8%
1946	20 215 200	24 696 949	81.9%
1951	19 670 655	24 530 523	80.2%
1956	22 138 046	26 772 255	82.7%
1958	21 026 543	27 244 992	77.2%
1962	18 918 154	27 540 358	68.7%
1967	22 910 839	28 242 549	81.1%
1968	22 500 524	28 178 087	79.9%
1973	24 299 210	29 883 738	81.3%
1978	24 658 645	34 424 388	71.6%
1981	25 182 623	35 536 041	70.9%
1986	28 736 080	36 614 738	78.5%
1988	24 472 329	36 977 321	66.2%
1993	26 860 177	38 968 660	68.9%
1997	26 649 818	39 215 743	68.0%
2002	22 186 165	36 783 746	60.3%

Germany

YEAR	TOTAL VOTE	REGISTRATION	VOTE/REG
1949	24 495 614	31 207 620	78.5%
1953	28 479 550	33 120 940	86.0%
1957	31 072 894	35 400 923	87.8%
1961	32 849 624	37 440 715	87.7%
1965	33 416 207	38 510 395	86.8%
1969	33 523 064	38 677 235	86.7%
1972	37 761 589	41 446 302	91.1%

YEAR	TOTAL VOTE	REGISTRATION	VOTE/REG
1976	38 165 753	42 058 015	90.7%
1980	38 292 176	43 231 741	88.6%
1983	39 279 529	44 088 935	89.1%
1987	38 225 294	45 327 982	84.3%
1990	46 995 915	60 436 560	77.8%
1994	47 737 999	60 452 009	79.0%
1998	49 947 087	60 762 751	82.2%
2002	48 582 761	61 432 868	79.1%

Greece

YEAR	TOTAL VOTE	REGISTRATION	VOTE/REG
1946	1 121 696	N/A	N/A
1950	1 696 146	N/A	N/A
1951	1 717 012	2 224 246	77.2%
1952	1 600 172	2 123 150	75.4%
1956	3 379 445	4 507 907	75.0%
1958	3 863 982	5 119 148	75.5%
1961	4 640 512	5 668 298	81.9%
1963	4 702 791	5 662 965	83.0%
1964	4 626 290	5 662 965	81.7%
1974	4 966 558	6 241 066	79.6%
1977	5 193 891	6 403 738	81.1%
1981	5 753 478	7 059 778	81.5%
1985	6 421 466	7 661 588	83.8%
1989	6 799 485	8 061 803	84.3%
1989	6 669 228	7 892 904	84.5%
1993	7 019 925	8 462 636	83.0%
1996	6 952 938	9 107 766	76.3%
2000	7 027 007	9 373 439	75.0%

Iceland

YEAR	TOTAL VOTE	REGISTRATION	VOTE/REG
1946	67 895	77 670	87.4%
1949	73 432	82 481	89.0%
1953	78 754	87 601	89.9%
1956	84 355	91 618	92.1%
1959	86 147	95 050	90.6%
1959	86 426	95 637	90.4%
1963	90 958	99 798	91.1%
1967	97 855	107 101	91.4%

Part III: The International IDEA Database: Voter Turnout from 1945 to 2003

YEAR	TOTAL VOTE	REGISTRATION	VOTE/REG
1971	106 975	118 289	90.4%
1974	115 575	126 388	91.4%
1978	124 377	137 782	90.3%
1979	126 929	142 073	89.3%
1983	133 764	150 977	88.6%
1987	154 438	171 402	90.1%
1991	160 142	182 768	87.6%
1995	167 751	191 973	87.4%
1999	169 431	201 525	84.1%
2003	184 813	211 289	87.5%

Ireland

YEAR	TOTAL VOTE	REGISTRATION	VOTE/REG
1948	1 336 628	1 800 210	74.2%
1951	1 343 616	1 785 144	75.3%
1954	1 347 932	1 763 209	76.4%
1957	1 238 559	1 738 278	71.3%
1961	1 179 738	1 670 860	70.6%
1965	1 264 666	1 683 019	75.1%
1969	1 334 963	1 735 388	76.9%
1973	1 366 474	1 783 604	76.6%
1977	1 616 770	2 118 606	76.3%
1981	1 734 379	2 275 450	76.2%
1982	1 701 385	2 335 153	72.9%
1987	1 793 406	2 445 515	73.3%
1989	1 677 592	2 448 810	68.5%
1992	1 751 351	2 557 036	68.5%
1997	1 788 997	2 707 498	66.1%
2002	1 878 609	3 002 173	62.6%

Italy

YEAR	TOTAL VOTE	REGISTRATION	VOTE/REG
1946	24 947 187	28 005 449	89.1%
1948	26 854 203	29 117 554	92.2%
1953	28 410 851	30 267 080	93.9%
1958	30 399 708	32 436 022	93.7%
1963	31 766 058	34 201 660	92.9%
1968	33 003 249	35 566 681	92.8%
1972	34 524 106	37 049 654	93.2%
1976	37 741 404	40 423 131	93.4%

YEAR	TOTAL VOTE	REGISTRATION	VOTE/REG
1979	38 112 228	42 181 664	90.4%
1983	39 114 321	43 936 534	89.0%
1987	40 599 490	45 689 829	88.9%
1992	41 479 764	47 435 964	87.4%
1994	41 461 260	48 135 041	86.1%
1996	40 496 438	48 846 238	82.9%
2001	40 195 500	49 358 947	81.4%

Luxembourg

YEAR	TOTAL VOTE	REGISTRATION	VOTE/REG
1948	77 865	84 724	91.9%
1951	83 613	92 110	90.8%
1954	170 092	183 590	92.6%
1959	173 836	188 286	92.3%
1964	173 702	191 788	90.6%
1968	170 566	192 601	88.6%
1974	185 527	205 817	90.1%
1979	188 909	212 614	88.9%
1984	191 651	215 792	88.8%
1989	191 332	218 940	87.4%
1994	191 724	217 131	88.3%
1999	191 267	221 103	86.5%

Malta

YEAR	TOTAL VOTE	REGISTRATION	VOTE/REG
1947	106 141	140 703	75.4%
1950	106 820	140 516	76.0%
1951	113 366	151 977	74.6%
1953	119 333	148 478	80.4%
1955	121 243	149 380	81.2%
1962	151 533	166 936	90.8%
1966	144 873	161 490	89.7%
1971	168 913	181 768	92.9%
1976	206 843	217 724	95.0%
1981	225 466	238 237	94.6%
1987	236 719	246 292	96.1%
1992	249 145	259 423	96.0%
1996	264 037	271 746	97.2%
1998	268 150	281 078	95.4%
2003	285 122	297 390	95.7%

Voter Turnout in Western Europe

Netherlands

YEAR	TOTAL VOTE	REGISTRATION	VOTE/REG
1946	4 913 015	5 275 888	93.1%
1948	5 089 582	5 433 633	93.7%
1952	5 501 728	5 792 679	95.0%
1956	5 849 652	6 125 210	95.5%
1959	6 143 409	6 427 864	95.6%
1963	6 419 964	6 748 611	95.1%
1967	7 076 328	7 452 776	94.9%
1971	6 364 719	8 048 726	79.1%
1972	7 445 287	8 916 947	83.5%
1977	8 365 829	9 506 318	88.0%
1981	8 738 238	10 040 121	87.0%
1982	8 273 631	10 216 634	81.0%
1986	9 199 621	10 727 701	85.8%
1989	8 919 787	11 112 189	80.3%
1994	9 021 144	11 455 924	78.7%
1998	8 607 787	11 755 132	73.2%
2002	9 515 226	12 035 935	79.1%
2003	9 666 602	12 076 711	80.0%

Norway

YEAR	TOTAL VOTE	REGISTRATION	VOTE/REG
1945	1 498 194	1 961 977	76.4%
1949	1 770 897	2 159 005	82.0%
1953	1 790 331	2 256 799	79.3%
1957	1 800 155	2 298 376	78.3%
1961	1 850 548	2 340 495	79.1%
1965	2 056 091	2 406 866	85.4%
1969	2 162 596	2 579 566	83.8%
1973	2 155 734	2 686 676	80.2%
1977	2 304 496	2 780 190	82.9%
1981	2 462 142	3 003 093	82.0%
1985	2 605 436	3 100 479	84.0%
1989	2 653 173	3 190 311	83.2%
1993	2 472 551	3 259 957	75.8%
1997	2 583 809	3 311 215	78.0%
2001	2 517 497	3 358 856	75.0%

Portugal

YEAR	TOTAL VOTE	REGISTRATION	VOTE/REG
1975	5 666 696	6 177 698	91.7%
1976	5 393 853	6 477 619	83.3%
1979	5 915 168	6 757 152	87.5%
1980	5 917 355	6 925 243	85.4%
1983	5 629 996	7 159 349	78.6%
1985	5 744 321	7 621 504	75.4%
1987	5 623 128	7 741 149	72.6%
1991	5 674 332	8 322 481	68.2%
1995	5 904 854	8 906 608	66.3%
1999	5 406 946	8 857 173	61.0%
2002	5 582 146	8 882 561	62.8%

Spain

YEAR	TOTAL VOTE	REGISTRATION	VOTE/REG
1977	18 175 327	23 616 421	77.0%
1979	18 284 948	26 836 500	68.1%
1982	21 439 152	26 855 301	79.8%
1986	20 489 651	29 117 613	70.4%
1989	20 788 160	29 694 055	70.0%
1993	23 907 495	31 030 511	77.0%
1996	24 985 097	32 007 554	78.1%
2000	23 339 490	33 969 640	68.7%

Sweden

YEAR	TOTAL VOTE	REGISTRATION	VOTE/REG
1948	3 895 161	4 707 783	82.7%
1952	3 801 284	4 805 216	79.1%
1956	3 902 114	4 902 114	79.6%
1958	3 864 963	4 992 421	77.4%
1960	4 271 610	4 972 177	85.9%
1964	4 273 595	5 095 850	83.9%
1968	4 861 901	5 445 333	89.3%
1970	4 984 207	5 645 804	88.3%
1973	5 168 996	5 690 333	90.8%
1976	5 457 043	5 947 077	91.8%
1979	5 480 126	6 040 461	90.7%
1982	5 606 603	6 130 993	91.4%
1985	5 615 242	6 249 445	89.9%

Part III: The International IDEA Database: Voter Turnout from 1945 to 2003

YEAR	TOTAL VOTE	REGISTRATION	VOTE/REG
1988	5 441 050	6 330 023	86.0%
1991	5 562 920	6 413 172	86.7%
1994	5 725 246	6 496 365	88.1%
1998	5 374 588	6 603 129	81.4%
2002	5 385 430	6 722 152	80.1%

Switzerland

YEAR	TOTAL VOTE	REGISTRATION	VOTE/REG
1947	985 499	1 374 740	71.7%
1951	986 937	1 414 308	69.8%
1955	998 881	1 453 807	68.7%
1959	1 008 563	1 473 155	68.5%
1963	986 997	1 531 164	64.5%
1967	1 019 907	1 559 479	63.8%
1971	2 000 135	3 548 860	56.4%
1975	1 955 752	3 733 113	52.4%
1979	1 856 689	3 863 169	48.1%
1983	1 990 012	4 068 532	48.9%
1987	1 958 469	4 125 078	47.5%
1991	2 076 886	4 510 784	46.0%
1995	1 940 646	4 593 772	42.2%
1999	2 004 540	4 638 284	43.2%

United Kingdom

YEAR	TOTAL VOTE	REGISTRATION	VOTE/REG
1945	24 117 191	33 240 391	72.6%
1950	28 771 124	34 412 255	83.6%
1951	28 596 594	34 919 331	81.9%
1955	26 759 729	34 852 179	76.8%
1959	27 862 652	35 397 304	78.7%
1964	27 698 221	35 894 054	77.2%
1966	27 314 646	35 957 245	76.0%
1970	28 386 145	39 342 013	72.2%
1974	29 226 810	40 072 970	72.9%
1974	31 382 414	39 753 863	78.9%
1979	31 233 208	41 095 490	76.0%
1983	30 722 241	42 192 999	72.8%
1987	32 566 523	43 180 573	75.4%
1992	33 653 800	43 240 084	77.8%
1997	31 289 097	43 784 559	71.5%
2001	26 365 192	44 403 238	59.4%

PRESIDENTIAL ELECTIONS

1945–2003

Part III: The International IDEA Database: Voter Turnout from 1945 to 2003

Austria

YEAR	TOTAL VOTE	REGISTRATION	VOTE/REG
1951	4 373 194	4 513 597	96.9%
1957	4 499 565	4 630 997	97.2%
1963	4 654 657	4 869 928	95.6%
1965	4 679 427	4 874 928	96.0%
1971	4 787 706	5 024 324	95.3%
1974	4 733 016	5 031 772	94.1%
1980	4 779 054	5 215 875	91.6%
1986	4 745 849	5 436 846	87.3%
1992	4 592 927	5 676 903	80.9%
1998	4 351 272	5 848 584	74.4%

Finland

YEAR	TOTAL VOTE	REGISTRATION	VOTE/REG
1950	1 585 835	2 487 230	63.8%
1956	1 905 449	2 597 738	73.4%
1962	2 211 441	2 714 883	81.5%
1968	2 048 784	2 930 635	69.9%
1978	2 470 339	3 844 279	64.3%
1982	3 188 056	3 921 005	81.3%
1988	3 141 360	4 036 169	77.8%
1994	3 193 825	4 150 000	77.0%
2000	3 200 580	4 167 204	76.8%

France

YEAR	TOTAL VOTE	REGISTRATION	VOTE/REG
1965	23 744 400	28 200 000	84.2%
1969	22 200 000	28 800 000	77.1%
1974	25 100 000	29 800 000	84.2%
1981	30 350 568	36 398 762	83.4%
1988	32 164 400	38 200 000	84.2%
1995	31 852 695	39 976 944	79.7%
2002	32 832 295	41 191 169	79.7%

Iceland

YEAR	TOTAL VOTE	REGISTRATION	VOTE/REG
1952	70 457	85 887	82.0%
1968	103 900	112 737	92.2%
1980	129 595	143 196	90.5%

YEAR	TOTAL VOTE	REGISTRATION	VOTE/REG
1988	126 535	173 800	72.8%
1996	167 319	194 784	85.9%

Ireland

YEAR	TOTAL VOTE	REGISTRATION	VOTE/REG
1945	1 086 338	1 803 463	60.2%
1959	980 168	1 678 450	58.4%
1966	1 116 915	1 709 161	65.3%
1973	1 279 688	2 688 316	47.6%
1990	1 584 095	2 471 308	64.1%
1997	1 279 688	2 739 529	46.7%

Portugal

YEAR	TOTAL VOTE	REGISTRATION	VOTE/REG
1976	4 885 624	6 477 484	75.4%
1980	5 834 789	6 931 641	84.2%
1986	5 939 311	7 600 001	78.1%
1991	5 099 092	8 235 151	61.9%
1996	5 762 978	8 693 636	66.3%
2001	4 468 442	8 932 106	50.0%

EUROPEAN PARLIAMENT ELECTIONS

1979–1999

Part III: The International IDEA Database: Voter Turnout from 1945 to 2003

Austria

YEAR	TOTAL VOTE	REGISTRATION	VOTE/REG
1996	3 928 538	5 800 377	67.7%
1999	2 865 977	5 847 605	49.0%

Belgium

YEAR	TOTAL VOTE	REGISTRATION	VOTE/REG
1979	6 485 994	7 096 273	91.4%
1984	6 431 574	6 975 677	92.2%
1989	6 168 130	6 800 584	90.7%
1994	6 537 968	7 211 311	90.7%
1999	6 686 222	7 343 466	91.0%

Denmark

YEAR	TOTAL VOTE	REGISTRATION	VOTE/REG
1979	1 794 614	3 754 423	47.8%
1984	2 032 386	3 878 600	52.4%
1989	1 812 680	3 923 549	46.2%
1994	2 113 780	3 994 200	52.9%
1999	2 021 922	4 012 440	50.4%

Finland

YEAR	TOTAL VOTE	REGISTRATION	VOTE/REG
1996	2 366 504	4 108 703	57.6%
1999	1 247 685	4 141 098	30.1%

France

YEAR	TOTAL VOTE	REGISTRATION	VOTE/REG
1979	21 354 582	35 180 531	60.7%
1984	20 911 350	36 880 688	56.7%
1989	18 675 569	38 348 191	48.7%
1994	20 590 577	39 044 441	52.7%
1999	18 765 259	40 129 780	46.8%

Germany

YEAR	TOTAL VOTE	REGISTRATION	VOTE/REG
1979	28 088 025	42 751 940	65.7%
1984	25 248 725	44 451 981	56.8%
1989	28 516 691	45 773 179	62.3%
1994	36 295 529	60 473 927	60.0%

YEAR	TOTAL VOTE	REGISTRATION	VOTE/REG
1999	27 472 760	60 766 241	45.2%

Greece

YEAR	TOTAL VOTE	REGISTRATION	VOTE/REG
1981	5 752 789	7 319 070	78.6%
1984	6 014 119	7 790 309	77.2%
1989	6 669 562	8 347 387	79.9%
1994	6 803 884	8 459 636	80.4%
1999	6 712 684	8 912 901	75.3%

Ireland

YEAR	TOTAL VOTE	REGISTRATION	VOTE/REG
1979	5 752 789	7 319 070	63.6%
1984	6 014 119	7 790 309	47.6%
1989	6 669 562	8 347 387	68.3%
1994	6 803 884	8 459 636	44.0%
1999	6 712 684	8 912 901	50.7%

Italy

YEAR	TOTAL VOTE	REGISTRATION	VOTE/REG
1979	35 822 170	42 193 369	84.9%
1984	37 061 545	44 438 303	83.4%
1989	37 719 017	46 566 688	81.0%
1994	35 505 023	47 489 843	74.8%
1999	34 910 815	49 309 064	70.8%

Luxembourg

YEAR	TOTAL VOTE	REGISTRATION	VOTE/REG
1979	189 126	212 740	88.9%
1984	191 623	215 792	88.8%
1989	191 354	218 940	87.4%
1994	198 370	224 031	88.5%
1999	185 768	216 512	85.8%

Netherlands

YEAR	TOTAL VOTE	REGISTRATION	VOTE/REG
1979	5 698 550	9 808 176	58.1%

Voter Turnout in Western Europe

YEAR	TOTAL VOTE	REGISTRATION	VOTE/REG
1984	5 300 856	10 476 000	50.6%
1989	5 249 337	11 121 477	47.2%
1994	4 133 309	11 620 300	35.6%
1999	3 544 408	11 855 000	29.9%

Portugal

YEAR	TOTAL VOTE	REGISTRATION	VOTE/REG
1987	5 638 225	7 787 603	72.4%
1989	4 151 139	8 107 694	51.2%
1994	3 044 001	8 565 822	35.5%
1999	3 460 777	8 572 953	40.4%

Spain

YEAR	TOTAL VOTE	REGISTRATION	VOTE/REG
1987	19 593 304	28 437 306	68.9%
1989	15 989 054	29 283 982	54.6%
1994	18 664 055	31 558 724	59.1%
1999	21 209 685	32 944 451	64.4%

Sweden

YEAR	TOTAL VOTE	REGISTRATION	VOTE/REG
1995	2 683 151	6 449 882	41.6%
1999	2 588 514	6 664 205	38.8%

United Kingdom

YEAR	TOTAL VOTE	REGISTRATION	VOTE/REG
1979	13 446 091	41 573 897	32.3%
1984	13 998 190	42 984 998	32.6%
1989	15 829 054	43 710 568	36.2%
1994	15 827 417	43 443 944	36.4%
1999	10 689 847	44 499 329	24.0%

Part III: The International IDEA Database: Voter Turnout from 1945 to 2003

Ranking table of vote to registration ratio by country, 1945-2003

A. National Parliamentary Elections

Country (no. of elections)	vote/reg %
Belgium (18)	92.5
Austria (18)	90.9
Italy (15)	89.8
Luxembourg (12)	89.7
Iceland (17)	89.5
Malta (14)	88.2
Netherlands (18)	86.6
Denmark (23)	86.0
Sweden (18)	85.7
Germany (15)	85.0
Western Europe - Overall	82.1
Norway (15)	80.4
Greece (16)	79.9
Spain (8)	75.7
Finland (17)	75.6
United Kingdom (16)	75.2
France (16)	74.8
Portugal (11)	73.6
Ireland (16)	72.6
Switzerland (14)	56.6

B. Presidential Elections

Country (no. of elections)	vote/reg %
Austria (10)	90,9
Iceland (5)	84.7
France (7)	81.8
Western Europe - Overall (43)	77.4
Finland (9)	74.0
Portugal (6)	69.3
Ireland (6)	57.1

Source: International IDEA.
Key: no.=number of elections.

C. European Parliament Elections

Country (no. of elections)	vote/reg %
Belgium (5)	91.2
Luxembourg (5)	87.9
Italy (5)	79.0
Greece (5)	78.3
Spain (4)	61.8
European Union - Overall (64)	60.6
Austria (2)	58.4
Germany (5)	58.0
Ireland (5)	54.8
France (5)	53.1
Denmark (5)	49.9
Portugal (4)	49.9
Netherlands (5)	44.3
Finland (2)	43.9
Sweden (2)	40.2
United Kingdom (5)	32.3

Sources

General Sources

The Administration and Cost of Elections (ACE) Project, 1999, a joint project between International IDEA, the United Nations and the International Foundation for Election Systems (IFES), <http://www.aceproject.org>

The Election Process Information Collection Project (EPIC Project), a joint project between International IDEA, the United Nations Development Programme (UNDP) and the IFES, <http://www.epicproject.org>

European Union official web site for elections to the European Parliament, <http://www.europarl.eu.int/home/default_en.htm>

International Foundation for Election Systems (IFES), Washington, DC, <http://www.ifes.org>

International IDEA, *Voter Turnout from 1945 to 1997: A Global Report on Political Participation,* 2nd edn (Stockholm: International IDEA, 1997), <http://www.idea.int/vt/index.cfm>

Inter-Parliamentary Union (IPU), Geneva, Switzerland, <http://www.ipu.org>

Reynolds, A. and Reilly, B., *The International IDEA Handbook on Electoral System Design* (Stockholm: International IDEA, 1997), <http://www.idea.int/esd>

Country-Specific Sources

AUSTRIA
Ministry of Interior, Electoral Office, <www.bmi.gv.at>

BELGIUM
Ministry of Interior, <http://www.belgium.fgov.be>

CYPRUS
Central Election Service, <http://www.cyprus.gov.cy>

DENMARK
Ministry of Interior and Health, <http://www.im.dk>

FINLAND
Ministry of Justice, <http://www.om.fi>

FRANCE
Constitutional Council, <http://www.conseil constitutionnel.fr>, and Ministry of Interior, <http://www.interieur.gouv.fr>

GERMANY
Federal Returning Officer, <http://www.destatis.de/wahlen>

GREECE
Embassy of the Hellenic Republic in Sweden, and Ministry of Interior, <http://www.ypes.gr>

ICELAND
Ministry of Justice and Ecclesiastical Affairs, <http://www.government.is>

IRELAND
Ministry of the Environment, Heritage and Local Government at <http://www.irlgov.ie>

ITALY
Ministry of the Interior, <http://www.interno.it> and University of Florence, Department for Political Science and Sociology, <http://www.unifi.it>

LUXEMBOURG
Chamber of Deputies, <http://www.chd.lu/default.jsp>

MALTA
Electoral Office, <http://www.opm.gov.mt>

NETHERLANDS
Ministry of Interior and Kingdom Relations, National Election Board, <http://www.minbzk.nl>

NORWAY
Ministry of Local Government and Regional Development, <http://odin.dep.no/krd/>

PORTUGAL
Ministry of Internal Administration, Secretariado Tecnico para Assuntos para o Processo Eleitoral (STAPE), <http://www.stape.pt>

SPAIN
Ministry of Interior, <http://www.mir.es>

SWEDEN
Swedish Election Authority, <http://www.val.se>

SWITZERLAND
Swiss Federal Chancellery, Section of Political Rights, <http://www.admin.ch/ch/d/pore/index>

UNITED KINGDOM
Electoral Commission, <http://www.electoralcommission.gov.uk>

Contributors

The Contributors

Tim Bittiger is currently Senior Programme Officer for Europe and Asia at IFES Ltd, a London-based provider of technical assistance in democracy and election processes worldwide. He previously worked with the Organization for Security and Co-operation in Europe (OSCE) and was head of the Local Government Department at the OSCE Presence in Albania until 2000. He is a graduate of Oxford University where he specialized in Modern European history and politics with a focus on South-East Europe.

Andrew Ellis, Head of the Electoral Processes Team at International IDEA in Stockholm, joined the Institute in September 2003. He has university degrees in mathematics, statistics and law, and a background in British politics as Vice Chair and subsequently Secretary General of the Liberal Party and Liberal Democrats. He has worked in many countries as a technical adviser on democracy and governance issues, and before joining International IDEA he was Senior Adviser for the National Democratic Institute (NDI) in Indonesia. He served as designer of European Commission technical assistance in Cambodia 1998 and acted as Chief Technical Adviser to the Palestinian Election Commission for the 1996 elections. He writes extensively, especially on Indonesian constitutional and electoral matters.

Maria Gratschew is a graduate of the University of Uppsala, Sweden. She joined International IDEA in 1999 as Project Manager responsible for International IDEA's Voter Turnout Project (see <http://www.idea.int/turnout>). She works mainly on voter turnout, election administration and compulsory voting issues in the Elections Team of International IDEA. Together with Rafael López Pintor she served as lead writer and editor for *Voter Turnout since 1945: A Global Report* (2002).

Rafael López Pintor is Professor of Sociology and Political Science at the Universidad Autónoma in Madrid, Spain, and is an international political consultant to the United Nations, the European Union and International IDEA, among other organizations. He has published a number of books and articles in the field of public opinion and elections in a variety of languages. His most recent studies are *Electoral Management Bodies as Institutions of Governance* (New York: UNDP 2000) and *Votos contra Balas* (Barcelona: Planeta, 1999).

Pippa Norris is Associate Director (Research) at the Shorenstein Center on the Press, Politics and Public Policy and Lecturer at the John F. Kennedy School of Government, Harvard University. She has published some two dozen books comparing gender politics, elections and voting behaviour, and political communications. Her most recent studies are *Digital Divide: Civic Engagement, Social Equality and the Internet Worldwide* (New York: Cambridge University Press, 2001); *Democratic Phoenix: Political Activism Worldwide* (New York: Cambridge University Press, 2002); and *Institutions Matter: Electoral Rules and Voting Choices* (New York: Cambridge University Press, 2003).

Richard Rose is Director of the Centre for the Study of Public Policy at the University of Strathclyde, Glasgow, an election consultant to the media, the Council of Europe and International IDEA, and a consultant on governance issues to the World Bank. He is the author of more than a dozen comparative works on parties and elections, including the *International Encyclopedia of Elections* (Washington, DC: CQ Press, 2000); the *International Almanac of Electoral History* (with Thomas T. Mackie, several editions); and *Elections and Parties in New European Democracies* (with Neil Munro, Washington, DC: CQ Press, 2003). His writings have been translated into 18 languages. He is a Fellow of the British Academy and the American Academy of Arts and Sciences.

Nina Seppälä is currently a doctoral researcher at Warwick Business School in the UK conducting research on business—government relations in countries with systematic human rights abuses. She has previously worked on democracy promotion for International IDEA and on training in peacemaking and preventive diplomacy for the United Nations Institute for Training and Research in Geneva.